Ni de Aquí,
Ni de Allá

A multi-perspective account of the Dominican
diasporic experience

-DWA PRESS-

DOMINICAN
WRITERS

NI DE AQUÍ, NI DE ALLÁ

DWA Press is an Imprint of Dominican Writers Assoc., a 501 (c)(3) non-profit literary arts organization founded in 2015 with the mission to support Dominican writers by providing them the tools and resources to become published authors.

Cover Art Design: Luciannys Camacho
Courtney Aucone- Copyeditor
Roberto Carlos Garcia & Roxana Calderón- Poetry in English
Nia Ita- Essays in English
Carisa Musialik- Poetry & Essays in Spanish

Print ISBN: 978-0-578-54396-3
EBook ISBN: 978-1-7352308-5-6

DWA Press:
An Imprint of the Dominican Writers Association
www.dominicanwriters.com
Email: info@dominicanwriters.com

Table of Contents

Ni de Aquí,
Ni de Allá

I was raised so damn Dominican.
Spanish my first language;
Bachata a reminder of the power of my body.
Platano and salami for years before I ever
tasted peanut butter and jelly sandwiches
If you asked me what I was, and you
meant in terms of culture,
I'd say Dominican, no hesitation, no
question about it.

Clap when you land, Elizabeth Acevedo

ESL - Luz Ozoria

I've learned to master
English like Sofia Vergara.
On good days, you can't even see
the accent clinging to the tip of my tongue,
but I'm running out of pages
and spaces, and storage to translate my traumas
first written in the language of my demons.
The same language mamá used to cast spells
on my wounds,"Sana, sana, colita de rana."
I go over every word with Merriam-Webster
and translate the stories I memorized in Spanish.

Not enough adjectives to describe the betrayal
of correazos for asking too many questions,
or the way agua de coco refresca hasta el alma
cuando no hay luz y el abanico no prende.
I fall short and every poem feels half done,
como que le falta algo,
como que le falta todo.

Hot Chocolate- Yohely Salazar

"Where are you from?!" She asks excitedly in that Valley girl accent I've come to expect in Los Angeles. My back is to her while I work, but I can see her reflection in the espresso machine. Her ash platinum hair resembles the thick cloud of steam coming from the frothing cup as I heat up some soy milk. I calmly mix in a bit of cinnamon.
She's nice, if a little clueless, but I'm not in the mood to answer with my usually flippant *"I'm American."* So, I say robotically,
"I'm originally from the Dominican Republic," since I know from experience this is what she wants to hear. Yet still I add, "but I also grew up in Massachusetts."

I add in the creamy milk to the chocolate syrup-filled cup as she completely ignores my New England childhood and focuses solely on her limited perception of me based on the origin, I've just told her:

"Ooh, Latina, you're so *spicy!*" she says as I shake in a little sea salt. I have barely said a word to this woman and yet I am *"spicy"* by virtue of my cultural background. My actual personality and who I am as a person hold no true weight. Since I am from a Latin American country I must, by default, be *"spicy."* I don't even like spicy things, much less love the idea of having that as my general descriptor.
I know from encountering outright bigotry that her excitement at my supposed and perceived fierceness comes from a place of true ignorant curiosity, not malice. I am not necessarily offended but it stings, nonetheless. I am automatically lumped into this stereotype having

2

barely opened my mouth. I have no discernible personality, and most importantly, I have no voice.

I smile without feeling it as I lightly put the plastic lid on the paper cup and hand her the hot chocolate, I've just made her. "That'll be $3.50, please." I've gone through this too many times and it's been too long a day for me to stand there and explain to her why her comments are problematic. If I had the energy, I might have actually taken the time to tell her how uncomfortable a descriptor "spicy" really was for me.

Whenever I had to meet a new person as a kid, my throat would close up and my palms would get disastrously sweaty. The sweat would drip down my fingertips and splash down to the ground. I never made friends, I inherited them. My sister, an outgoing, more talkative version of me, would collect them. Eventually, I would find myself surrounded by new friends I didn't really have to work to acquire. I had a strong personality, but my absurd shyness made it so I was the polar opposite of anyone's idea of a spicy Latina.

I was a quiet kid, constantly exoticized and subsequently reduced to nothing more than a condiment anytime I exhibited any level of emotion. It (restate what you mean by "It") made it difficult to come to my own conclusions about my identity. That confusion, married to the relentless (relentless how?) idea of "progress via assimilation," made it impossible to feel comfortable in my own skin. The complicated nature of all these things combined also made it difficult for me to feel at home in my new country.

Through it all, my mother was determined to make sure her children did not "lose" their culture and more importantly, their language. I couldn't speak Spanish without being looked at negatively by random neighbors and strangers, who would yell at my mother saying, *"This is America, speak English!"* I had to speak Spanish if I didn't want to be given *The Look*. That stern look was an essential part of my childhood. Despite my mother's solo departure to the States about a year after my birth in Santo Domingo, that look was one my siblings and I came to know and respect well, and one that she clearly learned from her mother.

I loved growing up in the Dominican Republic with my grandmother. However, when I was 13 years old, my mom, who was living in the U.S.

with my brother and sister at the time, did something unusual for a Dominican mother. Instead of just relocating me, she asked me point blank where *I* wanted to live. Although I desperately wanted to stay, I also missed my mother fiercely, and the idea of studying in the U.S. seemed incredibly appealing, so I chose to abandon the proverbial ship to join my mother and siblings stateside. Several years went by before I was able to see my *mamá* again.

It is amazing how many things can change in a handful of years when you're not looking. When I finally did go back nearly 7 years later, it was like stepping out into a parallel universe to what I'd had cemented in my heart and mind. more roads were paved, my old neighborhood was full of colorful houses, one right next to the other. There were no more montes or random cows crossing the street, but my face was reflected everywhere I looked; different, but all Dominican. I was back home.

There is very little I remember when I finally arrived at my grandparent's house, except that once I entered the heart of our home, I saw my grandmother in the middle of that kitchen where I proceeded to dissolve into a puddle of nothing, barely able to choke out my first face to face *'cion mamá,* in what seemed like forever. (This run on sentence needs to be broken up)

"Mi hija" she said softly as she hugged me to her smaller-than-I-remembered frame and commented on how I was both demasiado flaca and beautiful. That night, we worked on plumping me up with my first chimi sandwich in years. In between bites, we talked about all of the things and nothing at all, while the mysteriously tangy and savory chimi sauce dribbled down my chin. The evening was full of nostalgic chats, chimis, and sips of refreshingly sweet chinola juice. The perfect homecoming.

The next morning as she was toasting pan de agua con mantequilla, mamá tasked me with making a pot of hot chocolate to go with our simple breakfast. As I pulled out the preferred olla with the forever dented bottom, mamá stood there conspicuously watching me. Except for an occasional smile her way, I paid little mind to this and continued on with the task at hand. Having grown up in el campo, Mamá always found ways to bring some of those countryside elements to her home in Santo Domingo, and so every once in a while, she would have fresh milk delivered right to our city doorstep, like something out of a 1950's film.

And so with no knowledge of the logistics of how that fresh milk made it there, I found myself carefully measuring out the frothy, fragrant and creamy liquid into the dented pot.

As I unwrapped a block of Embajador chocolate—remembering when my sisters and I would steal into the pantry to sneak some of the grainy but somehow still smooth chocolate—Mamá moved from my right to my left, still observing me. When I added in the necessary palito de canela, mamá placed her semi-closed fist pensively over her mouth and chin. And when I was finished after a dash of salt and began to pour out the hot, chocolatey drink, she said: "¿qué te pasó por allá? Tú antes hacías las cosas con más confianza en tí misma... ¿a dónde se te fue ese fuego?

The irony floored me. I'd spent so long silently fighting others ignorantly calling me spicy only to have my grandmother tell me I had lost some of that very thing so many had claimed for me. Having spent so many years tempering down my "dominican-ness" in order to fit in, I had ended up potentially losing a piece of myself; a piece my mamá felt was missing the moment she laid eyes on me after so many years. Being from another country, I will always feel a little out of place in the United States. Having been away from home for so long, who I was in my native country was irrevocably changed. I am too Dominican and I am no longer Dominican enough.

Cacao Inmaduro - Astrid Ferguson

Yo soy como la mata de cacao,
I am like the Cacao tree.
Me sembraron en Santo Domingo,
they planted me in Dominican Republic.
Una campesina de El Cibao,
the bats that pollinated my branches
flew in from Haiti.

It takes 5-7 months for cacao fruits to ripen.
Once you cut the fruit open, you'll see five rows of white
kernels embedded in white pulp.
These nuts are removed and fermented
for 3-5 days to get rid of the pulp.
After this, the beans are dried slowly,
they oxidize and turn a dark brown color,
like growing in a Dominican Mother's womb
brewing the blood of an unwanted Haitian.
Mixing the dual citizenship of the dreamy "American" in a pilón.
The beginning of a good story, of not belonging here nor there.
Like the in-between chocolate powder that never oxidized
long enough for an award-winning cup of hot chocolate
served at Starbucks.

I changed food stamps into Spanish.
Too broke for Jordans, and too dumb and light for creole
delicacy, lambi guisado.
So, I settled for a front stoop in the Bronx,
and silent afros that never feared the wind,
I never had the long black straight hair
every salon overcharges for,
not its boundless length nor its blinding shine.

I'm always forgotten by Dominican guys because I'm more
light-skinned black than tanned mamasita.
Left alone and washed away whenever they mispronounced
My German name.

I think it was a joke,

6

a way for my father to say "You don't belong anywhere."
You're just a mix of everything no one would dare mix
on one plate.

Own this space,
que no es ni de aquí, ni de allá,
una mezcla de sazón y chocolate inmaduro.

La lengua - Sarah Bautista Suzaña

Cómo explicarle a alguien en inglés como tú,
mi isla, me haces sentir
¿como todos aplaudimos al aterrizar?
¿como cada rincón produce dulces y sazones?
¿como se nace bailando y comiendo mango?
que el tabaco se produce y se consume por la misma gente
no solo para aparentar,
donde con un hilo de coser y unos palos solo falta la funda para volar una
chichigua,
donde Toys R' Us no le llega ni a los tobillos a todas las latas abolladas
para jugar la placa,
donde usar zapatos es recomendable pero no mandatorio,
donde los locos son parte de la comunidad libre y todo el mundo los
conoce y los protege,
donde es sagrado bañarse en los ríos aunque no haya un camino con
letreros.

How do I explain in Spanish
the abundance of life existing in New York City 24 Hours a day?
that no one knows you or cares about you,
the city where you can be whoever whenever
for as long as you want,
the place where you can eat Colombian food for breakfast,
Chinese for lunch and Italian for dinner.
How to explain that no one cares about pleasantries or greetings?
How you can be sitting next to a millionaire on the subway
or learn Hindi for free from a lifelong friend.
How could you explain that not everyone has a portrait of Jesus
in their house, that people will come over and reject your food, they
never read the unwritten rule how that's the rudest
thing you can do ?

How do you express yourself accurately when the vocabulary
is so different,
where there isn't a direct translation for coño?
How do you properly explain how much you miss
a place that was only yours temporarily?
How you can never be American enough

NI DE AQUÍ, NI DE ALLÁ

because your last name is not Anglo Saxon
because your first language was not English ?

How do you live with your people's constant longing?
Your people that don't completely accept you because you have an
accent or don't know enough Spanish or are too Americanized,
your people that judge your openness,
your forgiveness,
your strength,
your people who are no longer on an island
but scattered all over the world singing
dancing and writing about this hybrid generation of lost souls
with no real motherland to call our own.

¡Canta Cigüa! - Mayelyn Perdomo

La Cigüa Palmera es
El ave nacional de la República Dominicana
The way the pigeon is
The official bird of NYC.

Me gustaría creer
That I am the Cigüa
That alighted upon
Its concrete.

Far from home,
But always perched
On the imaginary
Palm trees of my mind.

Las palmeras
Que me hacen tanta falta
When I step onto
Rockaway Beach;

Give me Juan Dolio
Boca chica
Playa Dorada
Cualquier malecón.

Mami and Papi's nests are
Back on the Island;
A southern migration
Every other summer.

Yo vuelo también,
Though I was born here
Porque la isla
Me llama a mí así:

When the steam of a wash and set
Drifts out of el salón on Grand concourse

NI DE AQUÍ, NI DE ALLÁ

I smell the colmado,
Hear motoras,
Saludo a la vecina,
Rocking en la galería

My feet touch dirt roads,
Saco agua del tinaco,
Sleep under mosquitero,
Y me siento at home.

Soy una cigüita americana
Acclimated to the States,
O una paloma dominicana
Visiting her grandparent's place.

However, you like it,
Como tú quieras,
Yo canto como la cigua
Y vuelo como las palomas.

Porque Quisqueya está en mí,
Y hasta en Nueva York me espera.

Where Snow Melts- Lorena German

1999

You pop the cap on the bottle and it sizzles. This heat in Santo Domingo makes you so thirsty. You're hanging out on the street, chilling with your cousin and his friends. The sun is blazing extra today. You take it all in. This is your first time out with your cousin because usually Mami is holding your hand like you're a baby. She's scared of you getting lost since these ain't your streets. You're old enough now to roam with your primo in this home away from home. His friends are funny and they even laugh at your jokes. Sometimes you wonder if it's pity laughter since you lack the words they use. Your Spanish is mostly used for asking things from Mami and Papi. They say "refresco" and you say "soda." They say "carajo" but your "r" doesn't roll, so you don't even say it. It's tough to know if they're cool or if hay interés. You wish that wasn't the case, but the thought still pops into your mind several times. It's so hot. They don't seem too bothered, but your shirt is sticking to you and you're sure the nail polish on your toes has melted into your socks. Why didn't you wear sandals?

You stop at the chimi truck on the corner. You finally feel like you're laughing *with* them. The cold glass soda bottle feels amazing in your hand because this heat is suffocating. You guzzle it down. You're halfway through when you realize they are staring at you. Your cousin and his friends all watch your americana self chug the Red Rock in this heat without even offering them a sip. This moment drastically separates you from them. One of them speaks up. "¿Tú te vas a tomar todo eso sola con nosotros aquí parados con la garganta seca?" In the United States, each of you would have had the cash to buy your own drink. You realize you are not home and that you have messed up. You ask the hombre

12

selling the drink to give you some cups while your cousin's friends give you disappointed looks and he tells you there are no cups. Damn. You realize you'll have to give them your bottle. Less than half is left. You return to the group. They're silent. You're silent. You hand your bottle to your cousin's friend. She drinks some and passes it on. You look at the cement floor, but it's as expected: hard and unforgiving.

1990

You remember sitting on your uncle's lap in his truck and watching the mujeres on the street as you drive by. Yes, he's driving and you're on his lap. This place is different but feels natural. The rice and beans are so fresh and here you aren't called picky. You eat what Tia makes and you love it. The fruit drips down your chin and the juices are the only thing that can quench your thirst. You play outdoors and you chase your cousins. You ask Mami, "Why don't we live here again?" This is a dream. You learn about Abuela's vida and Abuelo's zapatería and Tío's negocio. You meet primo's friends and they all love how cool your English is. They show you the alleyway and talk about playing outside in the rain. They have stories and you absorb them. You listen so intently that you can imagine them, and it's like they're yours too.

When Tío invites you to go with him to the colmado in his truck, to sit on his lap while he drives, you don't even answer, you just run.

And when you see those mujeres walking about, you take in the landscape. It is so different from Washington Street in Lawrence, Massachusetts. On TV all you see are white families in big houses with funny problems that never seem to unravel into any real chaos. In magazines, you turn the pages to see both blonde and brown-haired women, but always fair-skinned. They are petite. None of them has to worry about pants that fit the curves of their hips but are too big around the waist. And everybody on TV, in magazines, on the radio, and on the street speaks English. No one can talk like your Mami or your Abuelo. You are thinking all these things as you watch the mujeres walking in Santo Domingo and it hits you. You exhale a breath of relief. You realize they all have brown knees. Like you. Finally.

1987

You'll always remember this passport picture you took when you were four because you're headed on a plane now. You'll keep this passport picture into adulthood. You are about to leave the land that birthed you;

13

the land that you'll forever claim as home. The trees, the breeze that warmly caresses your cheek en el patio; ese queso, the Red Rocks, the dulce de leches, Tío y Tía, Abuelo and Abuela, prima, primo, all of them. They'll stay, behind. You decide to take your school uniform with you. You also take your notebook. You leave your muñeca with prima since she always wanted to play with it. No need to fight about that anymore. You wonder what channel the muñequitos are on and you hope you don't miss too many episodes. You'll find out that "El monito Quique" isn't showing where you're headed. Instead it'll be "Ducktales" about un pato misterioso. You wonder about the snow people talk about and how much of it you'll be able to hold in your hands. They say your fingers will freeze, but how could that be possible when snow melts?

You've packed it all. You packed the socks Tia gave you, the dress Abuela made for you and all the shorts, pants, and shirts you can manage. You certainly packed the soft blanket you have because they told you, "Allá hace frío." And it still feels like it's not enough. You want to cry but you're not sure that you're sad. You're not sure what or who you'll miss the most. You asked when you'll return but there was hesitation, looks, and tension so you stopped asking. They don't want to tell you what is evident: they don't know and it won't be for a long time. How will you make friends with americanos? Who will your amiguitas be? What will the house look like? What is clear is that you're from here, but soon, you will also be from there.

What you don't know is that time will move quickly and slowly; that chaos will be embedded in these memories because hindsight isn't always 20/20 when it comes to the details of things. One day you'll better understand some decisions made. You'll better understand how to appreciate the interruptions what do you mean by this? You might flesh out this particular thought a lil more and the sacrifices. As you attempt to assemble what time and distance have taken away, you'll always rest on the breeze that caresses your cheek as you arrive in the Aeropuerto Las Américas, a confirmation that you are, in fact, dominicana.

Not Your Typical Dominican York - Judy Fernandez Díaz

Off we went to a country I would learn to resent.

Where I went from *"tú si eres prieta"* to *"negra fina"*
when the boys found out I was born in the US.

¿Pero y tú viajas?
No lo pareces.

You don't dress like a Dominican York,
you don't look like a Dominican York,
you wear your poverty in a way
that makes others uncomfortable
and makes us question the American Dream,
where money grows on trees.

Meanwhile behind the scenes,
title loans and high interest debt
to finance a life in DR that's different
than the humble hard -working
reality lived in the States,
which keeps perpetuating
the myth of immediate wealth
to all those who reach its shore.

Para tapar las apariencias,
sin cargos de conciencia.

Meanwhile, me and my family living a lie,
we don't even try,
straight from the projects
we lived our truth
velcro sneakers
k-mart jeans
no name brands in sight
just the plight
of a lost teen

who dreamed
of returning to the US.

Three years later, I returned
to the country I missed, insulted for being a hick.
Talking too loud in school,
not being cool.
Wearing colorful shirts,
velcro sneakers,
K-mart jeans,
and not having the means
to fit in.

Niños cantores- Agueda Pizarro

Pasaba por el *Check -in* con sobrepeso en el corazón. Mi tía y yo habíamos llorado tanto en la fila que la azafata no mencionó nada acerca de las 5 libras adicionales en las maletas. Es que mi tía le había contado a la azafata que este era mi primer viaje, que me iba a estudiar a España, que me había criado mi abuela, su madre, que era la niña de la casa y que viajaba sola. Entre lágrimas relató que no teníamos familiares ni amigos por esos lares y que no conocíamos a mi futura compañera de piso; que podría ser un hombre encargado de una red de blancas o la sobrina de madre Teresa de Calcuta, pero con las oraciones de la familia esperaba lo segundo.

Luego de dejar las maletas y la historia de mi vida, nos encaminamos al *gate* correspondiente. Le digo que me preste el móvil y me le despego un poco. El número me lo sé de memoria, marco y espero que él conteste. No relataré aquí mi conversación, solo les diré que la idea de separarnos por mi viaje fue mía, nunca he creído en las relaciones a distancia. Como ya hice el viaje en el tiempo, les diré que esa ruptura sólo fueron palabras que sirvieron para que el pobre pudiera encontrar refugio en sus noches frías sin tener pleitos de cuernos que yo no fui capaz de poner y él sí. Igual seguíamos llamándonos y desde que saqué pie de mi media isla la finca tenía dueño.

Luego de la llamada, mi tía me mira como diciéndome «Solo tú crees que no sé con quién estabas hablando». Sigue dándome instrucciones de que hacer antes, durante y después del vuelo. En la puerta la abrazo y lloramos juntas un poco más. Sí, todavía teníamos lágrimas. En el avión yo era la carne entre dos personas y no encontraba cómo esconder mis ojos hinchados. En la cena ordené el vino blanco y de un trago me bebí toda la botellita, a ver si me dormía tranquila entre el dolor de cabeza, el miedo de mi primer vuelo y haber dejado atrás a mi familia y a mi primer amor.

Al día siguiente, a medida que iba despertando, me sentí cómoda y reconfortada, había olvidado donde estaba hasta que abrí los ojos. Cuando me despabilé, me encontraba acurrucada de mi compañero del asiento derecho, un señor mayor que por su nariz perfilada, moños buenos y tez pálida catalogué como español. Estaba despierto y yo le había mojado su hombro derecho de mis lágrimas de medianoche. Sí, lágrimas, no averigües tanto. El español estaba erguido en su asiento, pero no hizo gesto de darse cuenta que había despertado. Me sentí avergonzada por mi desliz. Sin hablar me fui enderezando en mi asiento, roja como un tomatico Barceló. Del lado izquierdo mi otro compañero abrió la ventana y ya podía ver tierra mientras el piloto anunciaba que comenzamos a aterrizar. ¿Has recorrido una bajaíta en bicicleta sin frenos? Bueno, pues así se siente el aterrizaje de un avión, multiplicado por mil sin contar con que una no tiene control de nada. En esta parte todo el mundo ora. Cuando esas gomitas tocan la pista de aterrizaje ahí tienes un aproximado de los pasajeros dominicanos por la cantidad de aplausos que se escuchan. Ahí juré nunca aplaudir en ningún vuelo, que vergüenza.

En la correa mientras esperaba mi equipaje evité al español como el diablo a la cruz, ni las gracias le di o me disculpé. Español, donde quieras que estés, gracias y dispénseme la confianza. Varios familiares me habían recomendado ponerle un lazo a la maleta de un color chillón para diferenciarla, y gracias a Dios lo hice porque habían pasado ya dos iguales, pero no eran mías. Cuando vi ese lazo rosado fucsia corrí a su rescate. Sacándola casi me voy de lao' y en Madrid no había buscón ni cibaeño enamorao' que me ayudara, tuve que sacar de abajo y hacerlo yo sola. En retrospectiva, eso debió ser una señal de lo diferente que serían las cosas aquí.

En la salida me encontré con mi compañera de piso, *aka* apartamento, que me hizo el favor de buscarme al aeropuerto. Les adelanto que no resultó ser ni monja ni traficante de mujeres y en cuanto tuve la oportunidad se lo hice saber a mi tía. Mi habitación era una caja de zapatos y mi cama twin se meneaba como si fuera un terremoto al más ligero movimiento. Teníamos un tercer compañero, un conejo de lo más mono llamado pepito. ¿Sabías que los conejos no comen zanahorias? para que veas hasta dónde llega el engaño de la infancia, gracias Warner Bros.

Se me salieron las lágrimas al escuchar como los españoles decían Burger King o Spiderman y ellos flipaban cuando les hablaba del parqueo, marketing e insistía en ver las películas con subtítulos. En serio nunca te has reído hasta que ves a Bruce Willis hablar con la Z.

Desde el principio fue difícil adaptarme a la población que me rodeaba. Mientras, en mi media isla, no pasa un día sin que encuentres quien te salude en la calle, sin encontrar a un nuevo primo o quien te oriente cuando buscas una dirección. En Madrid te dejaban con la palabra en la boca y seguían de largo y cuando osaban a responderte lo hacían como si estuvieran peleando; lo que hacía difícil detectar cuando estaban molestos contigo en realidad.

Yo siempre me sentí huérfana de museos. Son tantas las veces que puedes ir al museo del hombre dominicano a ver el mapa de la isla en relieve o al museo del ámbar a ver bichos embalsamados en su tumba y actuar sorprendida. Yo moría por las obras del renacimiento, arte moderno, pinturas de Monet, Picasso, esculturas en todas partes. Añoraba actividades culturales más variadas, ir al teatro, feria del libro, conciertos de artistas pop que no estuvieran en tiempo extra. Quería ver monumentos, grandes ciudades, viajar en tren, tomar vino al mediodía.

En esos aspectos Madrid fue un gran maestro, me dejó ver grandes obras teatrales a presupuesto de estudiante, más museos y esculturas por metro cuadrado que en ningún otro lugar. Ponía a mis pies viajes con los cuales solo soñaba gracias a las líneas aéreas de bajo costo.

Madrid me enseñó a cocinar, si es cierto que la comida allí era muy buena y barata pero llega un momento que tu origen aflora y el cuerpo te grita arroz, habichuela y carne, sancocho y fritos verdes. Solo en Madrid pagué 4 euros por un plátano y 3 euros por media libra de auyama descolorida.

Madrid me ayudó a conocerme a mí misma. Sabes cómo a veces dices "el dominicano es un escandaloso, donde quiera que llega grita, no habla en tono normal." y lo dices como que estás hablando de algo ajeno, sobre todo porque eres medio tímida y no te gusta andar voceando ni saludando gente en la calle. Pues en la calle María de Molina me brillaban los ojitos cada vez que identificaba un dominicano, y si lograba presentarme hablábamos como viejos amigos que se encuentran fortuitamente. Los sábados eran días de bachatas de amargue con la que daba serenata a los vecinos y hacia la limpieza. Ojo, sin echar agua, ya me habían advertido. Nunca fui más dominicana que cuando salí de mi tierra, nunca la amé y la aprecié más que cuando la tenía a 8 horas de distancia.

En algún momento nos toca hablar del sistema educativo y de la brecha tan amplia que tenemos respecto a los demás países. Mientras que nos apoyamos en lo teórico y en libros obsoletos, a mí me tocó estudiar con casos de estudios de empresas reales, artículos de economistas y participar en discusiones en clase sobre la economía actual, el mercado americano vs el europeo, la fluctuación del euro, la burbuja inmobiliaria en España y la tasa del paro, la más alta en 20 años.

La mejor maestra es la carencia porque lo que no tenemos en el 4% de educación lo tenemos en el 100% de resolver. Lo que otros te hacen en 2 horas un dominicano te lo hace en 30 minutos, y si no sabe nada del elefante te habla del mejor amigo del elefante, que será aquel animal del que más conozca y por ahí se va. Igual es hasta normal sentir a veces que perdimos el tiempo en la escuela y que faltaron herramientas y conocimientos por impartir.

Se hace evidente que fuimos colonizados por españoles, pues es el país con más bares per cápita y tomarse un vinito al mediodía es común en toda Europa. No importa la temperatura o lo poco de conocerse, siempre habrá un compañero de Málaga o Granada que tratará de resolver tus problemas o los suyos yendo de tapas por el centro.

Mi cabello, el cual desrizaba en ese entonces, recibió el cambio de brisita de lo más bien, sé puso más bonito y brilloso, no parecían moño' malo'. Sí, ya sé que no hay moño bueno o malo, pero así le decía en esa época.

Sí, ya acepté mis rizos. Por esa época tenía una amiga dominicana, una doctora que me vivía diciendo que me dejara mi pelo natural. Y yo nananina, cremita hasta la muerte. Si usamos la máquina del tiempo te digo que dejarme mi pelo como me lo mandó Dios fue lo mejor que pude hacer en mucho tiempo. Gracias Doctora.

Donde no hubo suerte fue con los chicos. Además de que todavía estaba enamorada de mi dominicano, ninguna relación va a prosperar si usted no tiene galantería, *aka* tigueraje, lo siento, pero no. *Next*.

Unos meses antes de navidad, como dominicana que se respeta, jocie' mi pasaje, lloré, rogué que me dejaran volver en vacaciones a mi media isla porque no concebía una navidad fría con vino y jamón serrano. Yo quería mi brisita pascuera, cerdo en puya y cuba libre en vaso *foam*. Los jueces de la suprema, y la familia mía deliberaban sobre levantar el pedimento de entrada, tenían miedo de que me amarrara a una palmera en Boca Chica y no regresara a terminar mis estudios.

Después de una navidad en Santo Domingo ¿Cómo es volver al frío? por respeto no describiré la experiencia, no te quiero hacer llorar, ya lo hice yo por ti. Pero uno llora, se lava la cara y vuelve arriba, a la lucha. En esos meses me tocó trabajar y es envidiable cómo se cuida al empleado, cero estrés y 100% respeto. Se gana mejor y se vive mejor, pero uno tiene el corazón lleno de palmeras y playas calientes, vecinos que nos conocen de vida privada y familiares que te ven como un bicho no importa la edad. Hasta el museo del hombre me hacía falta.

Ya terminado mis estudios, después de 14 meses, o sea 427días, o sea 10,248 horas era hora de volver a casa, al calorcito de mi media isla. Aun cuando ya había mandado cajas de libros a casa a la hora del *check- in* , tuve sobrepeso, pero igual me dieron el chance. Sí, sí, sí, sí soy una chica con suerte.

En el vuelo de regreso a casa no dormí de la emoción. A medida que se veía en el monitor como el avioncito se acercaba al caribe se sentían las voces tomar más fuerza, hablar más alto, reír de cualquier cosa. En la parte de atrás del avión, como si fuera la cocina de una guagua voladora, se reían a carcajadas, se hicieron cuentos colorao' y escuchaba bachata de Anthony Santos a todo volumen. Una azafata tuvo que ir al área a poner control y unos minutos más tarde se anunció por altavoz la suspensión de venta de bebidas alcohólicas.

Luego, lo que todos estábamos esperando, nos indican por altavoz que nos preparemos para el aterrizaje. Cierro la ventana por donde ya se ven las curvas de mi isla mientras a mis oídos lo invaden el cliqueo de los cinturones que uno a uno cada pasajero se tercia. Una señora sentada detrás de mí se encomienda a la virgen de la Altagracia para que ayude a ese piloto a que terminemos el viaje bien. Siento la fuerza que empuja el avión hacia la pista, los asientos tiemblan. Tengo el corazón en un hilo hasta que hacemos contacto con la pista.

Cual coro de los niños cantores de Viena cada pasajero con sus manos como instrumento canta la canción más dominicana que se pudo escuchar. Es la manera más pura de demostrar agradecimiento por llegar vivos y por tener la oportunidad de volver a su tierra. Cómo cambia la gente, cómo cambié yo.

Transcurridos 14 meses, o sea 427 días, o sea 10,248 horas entendí el por qué. Luego de 10,248 horas hice lo que no había hecho antes ni haría después con la emoción que toda mi dominicanidad me permitía:.

aplaudí.

End

Un cariñito en español - Bremda Acosta

Yo lo que quiero
Es un hombre que hable español
Nada más ni nada menos
Mi inglés machucado es para el trabajo
Para la gente grosera en el tren
Para el tipo de la frutería
Esa lengua se descompone al quitarme los zapatos
Se me calienta la frialdad de Nueba Yol
Se me deshace el moño rizado
Se me cae la vergüenza de lo mal pronunciado
Yo lo que quiero es un hombre que hable español
Que no le importe que el Bustelo sea espresso
Que me guarde cremora de todos los sabores
Que me haga un sancochito en febrero
Que de repente me jale a bailar un merenguito
Que me cuente de su niñez en Santo Domingo
Es que a ti no tengo que explicarte mi existencia
Contigo no hay que traducir el amor
A ti no hay que decirte como darme cariñito mi amor

Lengua - Roberto Germán

Mi batalla con el lenguaje
Is nothing short of complicado
Soy un poquito de todo
Pero completamente nada
Dominican made
American raised
Speaking a remix of español e inglés
Blending the flexibility of la tambora
With the upright stillness of an organ
Recreating the National Anthem
To a backdrop of palos
Mis palabras son inglés sin barreras
Pero mi español no es exactamente un poema
Instincts seem to be gearing this
Confused mind trying to punctuate its experience
Ponderin' thoughts of goin' down yonder
Así es como se habla en el pueblo de Samaná
Estoy cansado
However
Sigo caminando
Saboreando limoncillos en Haina con los campesinos
O si no
Me puedes encontrar en el Boys' Club
Jugando baloncesto with my boys
Listen to our speech
A handful of arroz blanco
A handful of con-con
Chicken noodle haikus for the soul
Sancocho, a word for ears that love to look
Add a bit of sazón to make my adjectives more tasteful
Cause that's my tongue
Mi estilo de hablar
Posiblemente refleja la calle
Yo pienso en nada y en todo
Mi lengua es el ritmo de la noche

NI DE AQUÍ, NI DE ALLÁ

Mi lengua es el brillo del sol
Mi lengua es una mezcla de colores
Tengo el poder de predicar palabras profundas
Mi lengua son los gritos de nacimiento
Y también
De la muerte
Mi lengua es…
Un poema
Una canción
Un abrazo
El amor
Mi lengua

Ei problema mayoi - Yoseli Castillo

No señoi. No son la ONG, no.
Son utede mimo que lo dice con oigullo
« ¿Yo? yo no odio a to' lo haitiano pero ute nunca me va a vei a mí
donde un doctoi haitiano. Mejoi me muero »
No son la ONG, no señoi. Somo nosotro mimo cuando no graban poi la
inteinet diciendo que se mueran to y que se vayan to. No son la ONG, no.
Somo nosotro lo que salimo en la televisión diciendo que toa la mujere
tan pariendo, que tan llenando ei pai de to eso bicho pero entoce le
pagamo chele poi un trabajo que vale mile. Y si no pintan la casa to ei
dia lo dejamo sin comei y si le damo un tajo se lo cobramo como si fuera
bité encebollao. Eso no lo jace la ONG, no señoi.
Somo cuipable lo que lo contratamo poique ei dominicano no echa día,
ni en la finca, ni poniendo blo poi treciento o quiniento peso ai día
poique eso no e cuaito. No son la ONG, no.
Somo nosotro que no jaitamo de decí que to ello quieren vení ai paí pa
gobeinaino.
Ese e ei embute ma grande de to , dede ei 1844, epeciaimente cada ve
que ai eleiccione.
¿Utede no saben que ello fueron lo que no liberaron de Francia y Epaña,
que dei 1492 no tuvo eclavo? y como quiera no quisimo la
independencia, queríamo segui siendo un blanco eclavo que un negro
liberao, igualito que ahora. Todavía tenemo ei mimo problema. Ninguno
queremo sei negro. To queremo sei blanco, ya sea de Epaña, Francia,
Alemania, Suiza o Gringolandia. Eto e lo que se llama una contradicción,
to lo medio blanco son eclavo de su ignorancia. Ei único libre e ei negro
que sabe su condición de vítima jodía y abusá y se queja y lucha poi su
liberación, poi mejorai la condición de su raza día a día, encontra dei
vecino racita o ei gobieino nacionalita o la iglesia capitalita y maivada.
No son la ONG no. Somo to lo que dicimo que somo puro dominicano.
A vei, ¿qué je eso? ¿Nacei allá? ¿Comei plátano? ¿Hablai españoi
dominicano? ¿Sei medio blanco? Vamo a pensai aigo, ¿de dónde viene
ese nacionalimo jabao? ¿Se preocupan lo rico de veida poi habei o no
habei nació en ei patio, poi comei mangú con saichichón o poi hablai
epañoi dominicano? No. Claro que no. To eso degraciao, que con to han
acabao dede que Colón se peidió en ei Cibao, han nació o viven ma fuera
que de ete lao, comen de to lo manjare importao, hablan dique catellano
con inglé o francé o alemán meclao y claro, no se meclan con ninguno

que de África haya llegao. Entonce compai no me diga a mí que son la ONG la cuipable de que aiguno de nosotro defendamo a lo negro de aquí y lo de Haití. Aiguno de nosotro hemo vivío y aprendío y reflecionao. Sí to nosotro, no matamo a balazo o a machetazo, to lo blanco de la conquita y lo importao no tienen que hacei na' pa' seguí pisoteándono y robándono. Nosotro mimo no etamo acabando. Ello siguen ahí, en ei cojollito, echándose freco a nuetro cotao. ¡Ya ta bueno, carajo! Tenemo que depertarno dei sueño blanco latinoamericano.

Saudade/Anhelo- Lourdes A. Gautier

The American Airlines check-in at Newark Airport was crowded. I never checked luggage before, but traveling with two boys ages eight and ten, and the expected gifts for *la familia* made it necessary to take a large suitcase. There would be no rolling a small bag off the plane and bypassing the baggage carousel this trip.

"Mom, why are those people taking televisions on the plane?" asked my ten year old son, Justin.

I looked around me. Dozens of oversize suitcases and boxes holding all manner of appliances inched toward the check-in counter. Most people were speaking Spanish in rushed voices as they tried to figure out how to get their luggage checked in without paying overweight fees.

No one was dressed in the uniform of shorts or sundresses and sandals popular with visitors to a Caribbean island. Everyone had on closed toe shoes and slacks; dresses for the ladies and nice shirts and pants for the men. Even the kids were neatly dressed as if they were going to school or to church. It was 1991 and people still dressed up to go home. This plane wasn't going to Punta Cana, where *Norte Americanos* would transfer from the airport to a resort and not have to mix with the locals except for getting their food or having their rooms cleaned.

"Everyone takes gifts home for their families and the boxes will go in the cargo hold" I replied hoping that would be the end of the question and answer, period.

28

NI DE AQUÍ, NI DE ALLÁ

I disliked check-in and this looked like an exceptionally long line. We had arrived at the airport with an hour and a half to spare, but if everyone in front of us had to redistribute the contents of their bags it was going to be a close call.

"Do you think we'll miss our plane?" My eight-year-old son, Nick sounded worried. I knew my boys were confused about the abrupt decision to take them out of school and head off to visit family they had never met. I was sure they had somehow picked up on the vibe that I was oozing. If all went well, I planned on not returning to the United States. The last three years of my marriage had been a hellish experience. And years of never feeling like I belonged in the U.S. all converged to make me think that moving back to where I was born was the answer to getting out of this nightmare.

Two weeks ago, my mother had managed to overcome her resentment towards the family she had left behind in Santo Domingo. She gave me a message and a telephone number. My uncle was dying and wanted to see his niece before he checked out of this world. I held on to the piece of paper with the long-distance number for several days. Slowly, an idea began to germinate. Even after more than thirty years, I still felt that I didn't belong in the U.S. Maybe I should go back home, I thought to myself. Except for my mother, I had no family in New Jersey, and from what I could remember, there were tons of cousins and at least two uncles in Santo Domingo. For years, this sense of longing for a home, of belonging somewhere, was taking root in me. I was never comfortable when people asked me where I was from because they almost always meant where did I live or grow up. I always thought it should refer to my place of birth. Perhaps I was longing for a place that only existed as an imaginary memory.

On the third day of holding on to the slip of paper with the unfamiliar number and area code, I was feeling particularly desperate about my lack of roots. At 2:35 in the afternoon, before I had to pick up the boys from school, I reached for the telephone, dialed the international code, the foreign area code, and then the number. After five rings someone picked up the phone.

"*Hola, me llamo Lourdes. Soy la hija de Sylvia. ¿Puedo hablar con tío Victor?*"

And just as if it had been only a week since I'd last called, instead of the reality which is that I had never called, the voice (person) sounded happy to hear from me and went to get Uncle Victor. I was glad that whoever picked up the phone understood me when I gave my name and said that I was Uncle Victor's sister's daughter, his *sobrina*

I could hear the sounds of someone running, excited voices, and then the slow, methodical steps of someone that seemed laced (wrought) with pain. I began to panic. When was the last time I'd had a conversation in Spanish with anyone? I never felt completely comfortable on the phone, even at my most fluent. What if I sounded like a complete idiot? I wouldn't be able to revert to English, as I was sure no one in the house spoke it. These were people who'd never left the island.

"¡Sobrina! ¿Cómo estás?" Uncle Victor's voice sounded like a male version of my mother's voice as he asked me how I was doing.

After exchanging the usual pleasantries, I got to the point. I asked if I could could I come to visit right away, in the next couple of weeks. Maybe it was the three lost decades; or the knowledge that he had a limited amount of time left thanks to the cancer spreading through his body, but he said yes, even before checking with his wife. His goddaughter/niece and her two small children were welcome to come as soon as they could.

I knew that my sons would be overwhelmed staying in a strange place with people with whom they couldn't communicate, so I carefully suggested that we stay in a hotel. As soon as the details were confirmed, I called the airline and got three tickets. I got roundtrip tickets, not wanting to alert anyone of my proposed plan to run away for good.

I spent the next few days shopping for gifts for people I had never met or had not seen since I was just a child, younger than Nick.

The plane had a party atmosphere. Someone asked me how often I went home and was surprised when I admitted that the last time I was in Santo Domingo was over thirty years ago, when my mom moved us to New York City.

"Ay, hija, you won't remember anything then," they were quick to tell me. "Everything has changed so much."

The flight was just long enough to allow for time for me to worry about how I was going to relate to the blood relatives, who were strangers to me. I was unsure of how I was going to bridge the gap between my U.S. born and bred sons and their relatives. What would they talk about? Of course there would be questions about my mother. How could Sylvia have turned her back on everyone and on her country, her *patria*, without even a look back?

On some level, the airplane filled with Dominicans, making their twice or more per year pilgrimage home started to feel like home. Rarely have I ever been in the midst of so many people who looked like me or who spoke my first language. Even though I wasn't always comfortable communicating in Spanish, the sound, the words, and the way you could alter the meaning of anything by adding syllables that were sweet to the ear gave me a sense of my history.

Before we knew it, we were landing at *Las Américas International Airport*. For years, my mother warned me that I might be detained if I ever returned to the Dominican Republic.

Whenever I asked if we could visit, her response was "No. Your father would take you away from me as soon as we landed." This was said in a tone that made it clear the subject was closed for discussion. "He never gave permission for me to take you out of the country."

Although I felt my mother was exaggerating, I finally gave up trying to convince her to take a trip to Santo Domingo when I entered high school. By then, I was busy trying to eradicate the "Dominicaness" from my persona. A couple of years ago, we got news that my father was dead. The last threat that I would be detained if I returned home was gone.

The tropical air assaulted my senses the moment we stepped into the airport. Everyone looked like they might be related to me. How was I going to pick out my cousin? I spotted Eduardo within seconds and there was no question that he was my first cousin. The tilt of the head, that half smile and familiar facial structure reminded me of my mom. I figured

that picking us out of the crowd wouldn't be that hard. I exuded East
Coast USA with my
understated attire and two Americano, pale children who were dressed
like they were going to a Caribbean resort.

"Hola Lourdes, ¡aquí!" Eduardo waved to get my attention. He
hugged me like it was a routine thing to pick me up at the airport. His
government connections got us quickly through customs and connected
with our luggage.

Eduardo took us directly to his father's house. As soon as I saw
Uncle Victor, I knew this would be my first and last visit. The family
resemblance to my mother was painful to see in someone ravaged by
cancer. I held on to my uncle a little longer than necessary, almost as if
we needed to make up for three decades of missed hugs and kisses. He
was my godfather and my uncle.

"Pero que linda es mi sobrina," Uncle Victor spoke in his deep,
melodious voice that immediately reminded me of my mother. "Dejame
ver mis sobrinos." He turned his attention to Justin and Nick. My sons
didn't quite know what to make of all the attention they were getting
from these strangers. Somehow, they knew that it was an important
moment for their mother, and so they bravely reached out to shake the
hand of this man who was clearly in pain, but trying not to show it.

For the next week, I got a taste of what it would be like if I moved
to Santo Domingo. The taste, though interesting, wasn't familiar enough
for me to want a steady diet of it; I often found myself choking. Instead
of the carefree island life I had romanticized in my daydreams of running
away from New Jersey, there were too many rules to follow, thanks to
my family's position, and the almost colonial atmosphere of the capital
city.

I'd traveled through many foreign countries, and was used to taking
public transportation and getting around on my own. Here we were,
virtually prisoners. My family wouldn't let us travel through the city on
our own. We were always waiting for someone to send a car for us. It
wasn't safe, they kept saying.

Justin and Nick had willingly accompanied their mother on this
journey because they imagined it would be all about the beach, sand and

surf (the switiching between 2nd and 3rd person narration is starting to get confusing…),. After all, they had spent time in Bermuda and thought that all island visits were the same. It turned out that there was no beach onto which they could roll out of their hotel beds. Santo Domingo was a city and no one was dressed in sandals, shorts or resort wear. The *malecón*, the walkway along the water, provided a beautiful view, but no access to swimming. And in any case, no one in the family would allow us to take a stroll along the water's edge.

While I was growing up, my mother loved to recount tales of how she would stroll along the *malecon* with her own mother, or some other family member sent to provide her with a chaperone. Young men and women would catch each other's attention and flirt under the watchful eye of family. Now that I was finally here, I tried to imagine my mother as a teenager, enjoying the beauty of the island. Instead, all I saw was an environment that was like a billboard for the haves and the have nots.

During one of the visits to my uncle's home, I found myself alone with *tío* Victor. The kids were playing in the backyard with their new cousins and my uncle's wife had quietly disappeared to give us time alone. He was a lawyer who had almost become one of the disappeared during the Trujillo regime. There were so many questions I had but didn't know how to ask, such as why my mother had distanced herself from all of her family.and why she denounced all of them and the country as the worst place on earth. News of her father's death a few years ago sent her into inconsolable grief. The dichotomy of these emotions had always perplexed me.

My uncle and I only had fifteen minutes to talk, but it was enough for me to realize that there were issues I would never be able to understand, and that this island home, the place I was from, was not what I hoped it would be. There was no sanctuary for the lost. I would always just be a visitor.

Before heading to the airport to return to New Jersey, my sons and I stopped by my uncle's home to say good-bye. As I held on to this man who was at once familiar and yet a stranger, I knew it would be our first and last meeting. In some ways, we were so much alike. Those precious few minutes were enough for me to know that we would have gotten into so much trouble fighting the questionable politics of our country together. Perhaps it was best that I hadn't grown up in Santo Domingo.

Uncle Victor managed to get to the doorway to wave good-bye as the car pulled out of the driveway. It was the first time I'd seen him stand up. Within seconds, I was overcome with a sense of loss as I watched my uncle, *mi sangre*, emaciated from cancer raise his arm to send us off. I didn't want anyone to see the tears that streamed down my face. My uncle's wife, who was seated next to me saw, and reached over to take my hand.

There was no way to understand these emotions or to find a rational explanation. I knew at that moment that I would lose my uncle to his disease, and that I'd also lost something that perhaps never existed; a country to call home.

*Saudade....a Portuguese word for a sadness for something that is missing; deep, sad longing for the motherland.

Una dominicanyork aprende a jugar domino de verdad - Greisy Genao

"Mira. Muchachita. Pon atención porque
lo Americano a vece' no entienden eta' vaina.

Si come cabeza, es porque no te quedaba de otra.
Si trancas, es para la victoria.
Si te queda con toda la ficha en la mano,
~~espero que~~ es porque no te dejaron jugarla.
Siempre tranca a blanco, y nunca, nunca pase a tu frente."

We are playing to the 200.
If you eat your head, you were left no choice.
We are playing to the 200.
If you lock the game, it is for victory.
If all your tiles are in your hand, they didn't let you play.
Always lock on white if you can, and never, never
let your partner skip.

We are playing to the 200.
If both tails are the last tile played, capicúa.
Banda if no one can play on either side.
I know a guy who knows a girl from Moca, who knew
a guy who got killed over a game in a Queens basement.
Chivo if a wrong tile is placed and no one notices.

We are playing to the 200.
No table talk.
Don't look at your partner in the eyes.
I know a guy who knows a woman whose
102 year old husband plays every night. He knows
his own name and drank milk with Trujillo.
Sometimes he loses.
For example, if your partner plays the six,
either give her another six or leave it alone.

NI DE AQUÍ, NI DE ALLÁ

We are playing to the 200.
If you can't play after the first tile is put down,
it is 25 points to the bad guys.
I know a 16 year old who has never lost a game.
I know a woman who can count the tiles with her eyes closed.
If the table is full of women, a generational curse has been broken.

Where Are You Now Grandma, if Paradise Was by Your Side? (An Ode to Maria Celeste Llanos)
– A.M Shanti

~~Anytime that~~ When you arrive, I land.
An Island at your feet brushing passed
the ocean to crawl on flattened trees.

We gave in to a city, left the soft velvet green.
I land heavy on your belly.
Our sleep tucked in a canopy.

Abuela, can you hear me?
You are flower field - nightgown city.
Summer song spills through our windows
a sandbox of island living.

~~Y~~ou will remember me this size, a seed, soiled by the city
taking tiny steps out of our small apartment living.
Forgetting my tongue at the table, my teeth chewing
on the muscle memory of language.

¿Cómo se dice abuela?

Before your breath blows to breeze,

Que no te olvides de mí.

We're Out of Ketchup– Jarol Fabio

Everyone's familiar with that ubiquitous cluster-fuck scene in the movies that captures the "New York Minute":

The main character is standing still in the middle of Grand Central station, as the world around them moves by in highspeed; those around zooming-by in concentric blurs,—illustrating the fast pace and urgency seemingly demanded of anyone who chooses to call this city home.

I don't know how old I was or even which particular film it was when I saw this scene for the first time. Imagine me, my twenty year old native New Yorker self, standing in the middle of Grand Central Station during rush hour, playing out this very scenario.

I'd been working as a data entry analyst at the same investment consulting company since I was seventeen. My main responsibilities consisted of inputting and updating sensitive financial information on behalf of our campaigns and their investors.

I would usually leave the office at around 5pm, but because I had class I asked my supervisor if I could leave a bit earlier, in order to make it for my six o'clock class. I was pursuing an associate degree in International Business at Berkeley College, the for-profit, highly advertised business school whose only requirement was that you have either the funds to finance its tuition or the willingness to be preyed upon by any number of high-interest loan companies. Yes, that Berkeley College, not to be confused with the prestigious music school in Massachusetts, which I was often wrongly praised for attending.

A few months back, I decided to withdraw from the originally intended Bachelor's Degree track of the same program. I did this in part due to my eventual disinterest in finance, having worked on the surface area of that industry shortly after graduating high school, but mostly because of my lifelong inability to do math. To this day, when the brunch bill comes around and someone at the table shouts, "don't forget to calculate tax and tip!" I unlace my shoes and remove my socks; needing my toes to finish the calculation I started up above with my fingers.

This particular class was at its main campus in Midtown. At around 4:45 pm, I finished updating my last account and begin to gather my belongings at 17 State Street. Through the panoramic 10 floor-to-ceiling windows that cover our floor, I see that it is pouring outside. I ask my co-worker, Shelita, who is about thirteen years older than I was, if I could borrow her umbrella. I ask knowing good and well that she has anywhere from three to five others of which she kept underneath her desk. She is a mom of two and had been so for about six years. This gives her mastery over planning ahead and always being prepared. I take advantage of this daily.

Before there was Amazon, there was Shelita's desk. That is to say that anything that you might need, Shelita had it—within arm's reach. She regards me as a young brother of sorts. I could always tell when Shelita was going through stuff with her kid's father. He wasn't in the picture per se—they were separated. So instead, he provided financial and emotional support at his convenience. Some days she would arrive at work, visibly out-of-it—eyes puffy, a discernable gloom, unlike her usual cheerful self. A dispute with him during the night before would remove the soothing squeeze from her hugs the next morning.

On such days, she'd plop down into her seat and emphatically place the mommy Ziploc snack baggies on her desk, which she clearly intended for her kids' lunchboxes.. With a deep sigh, she would hide her face in the palms of her hands, defeated with disappointment and shame for having brought the snacks, baggies, w.e. with her into the office instead. I, being the kind-hearted and supportive colleague whom she would confide her most personal hurdles in that I am, tried to wipe the excitement off my face as I reached for the goldfish crackers and fruit gummies. As I gorged at my desk miles away, Shelita's children would frown upon opening their lunchboxes, finding only their sandwiches—

when the teacher permitted the class to enjoy their 10 minutes of snack time.

I cut through Bowling Green Park, taking my usual route to the 4-train. The rain is coming down on a diagonal due to the strong wind outside. My fellow commuters and I use our umbrellas more as shields than as tarps, as we blindly zig-zag and at times crash into one another. It's a fairly quick 10-minute ride from Bowling Green to Grand Central Station. On the train now, packed with the wet working class, I wedge my hand between two people and hold onto the pole. Today I am muh'fucking tide! I really am. It feels as if I'm a towel, and life is this Eastern-European heavyweight-lifter named Vladmir, who is ringing the everlasting fuck out of me—nearly dry. I'd been up late the night prior, studying for a bunch of exams coming up. I'm honestly just hoping that I can make it through this three and a half hour class from which I'll take the train uptown and either get started on a new assignment, or complete an existing one. Meanwhile, some of my classmates had gone to school earlier today and were probably just now completing their assignments. They would be in bed fast asleep long before I would get off the train on Dyckman Street at around 10:15pm.

I am not bitter. I'm not jealous of my peers for being able to enjoy more free time, or money for that matter; less still am I looking down on my own mother's socioeconomic status, and my modest upbringing. I'm just having a tired and wet day. The train continues to loudly make its way underground toward Grand Central Station. I begin to reflect on some of the friends I've made at Berkeley.

Take Mo for instance, who is from the South of France and whose parents, selfmade, fared well for themselves financially, having multiple investments and businesses. They were able to fully finance Mo's education both in England and now, in New York. On one occasion a few semesters back, out of punishment for going down 3-points in his GPA, who forbade him? forbade him from withdrawing anything more than $800/week from his (their) bank account. He was distraught and began to recall growing up in a refugee camp.

Then there is Gauté, from Norway, one of the most progressive and successful socialist countries in the world. Gauté's education both at home and abroad will be reimbursed by the government upon completion of his studies; not to mention that students receive a national stipend to cover reasonable living costs. In essence, you didn't pay to go to school. Rather, the government paid you to go to school. "I'm sorry. Do you want to run that by me again?," I ask Gauté one sunny spring afternoon, as we sip our coffees in Bryant Park, waiting for our next class. He indulges me. I begin wondering how much time I have before my next class to add eight inches to my height, dye my hair blond, change my relationship with the cold, and check non-stop flights to Oslo.

I begin losing myself in thought until I remind myself that I am no stranger to this "difference". I had been exposed to a similar narrative when I first entered high school in New York City. I didn't end up going to George Washington High school, the zoned school in my neighborhood of Washington Heights, whose student body, not unlike myself, came from low-working class families. Instead, my name was selected from a lottery system through the board of education. I was to attend the High School for Environmental Studies, one of the best public High Schools in Manhattan at the time with a much more diverse student population than what I had grown up with. Some of the students came from middle and upper-middle-class families, whose only reason for public schooling came from their parent's decision that it would better serve the development of their children in a more diverse social environment.
I make my way up the escalators and through the numerous corridors, which collectively spill into the domed celestial ceiling at the heart of Grand Central Station. I stand still, no longer reflecting on what kind of upbringing my wealthy friends and classmates throughout the years had had. Instead, my mind redirected itself to my own upbringing and narrative.

Here I am in real life. The focal character in this cameo shot— standing still in the middle of Grand Central Station, as all of New York City's most ambitious zoom-by in suits and heels, chattering into their cellphones. I take a quick breath, close my eyes, and bring myself to reflect on what it was like growing up in a different part of this city, in this very borough to be exact; Only a few miles up north from this train station with its endless commotion and chaos. Just a few train stops away but it might as well have been a whole different world. That's what growing up in Washington Heights was like. Much like the downtown metropolis I had grown to be a part of up north; In my neighborhood we, too, had noise, views, and smells, but they were different. They were a special kind of different.

Washington Heights is a microcosm of the Dominican Republic. Along with the island's various regionalisms—(Capitaleño, Cibaeño, Santiaguero, Banilero, etc...), then having that collective interweave itself into the fabric of the U.S It is genuinely a wonderful experience to be a part of a culture within a culture as it morphs itself and becomes its own peculiar and precious hybrid of language, accent, and nuance. For example, "Pero like....the thing is that..." I can't tell you how many times I've gone back to the island and have said something that I believed to be Spanish, only to find out that it's some combination of Spanish and English, probably conceived in The Heights. Take, for instance, Factura, which means bill or invoice. Factura put on its USA cap one wet autumn morning, went down to City Hall and decided to change its name to Bilés. Washington Heights is truly a wonderful place. You get two tickets for the price of one.

As my stillness grew, the noise of the echoing hall of Grand Central quickly faded.

—

Getting ready for school during my childhood, for the most part, played out like this: at around 7 am, my mother would come into the room of our one bedroom apartment on Audubon Avenue and click on the TV to either Nick Jr. or PBS. To credit her kindness, my mother never woke us up in the traditionally traumatizing fashion many Dominican parents across the world would wake their kids for school. That is to say that she didn't practically kick-down the door, SWAT-style, and clap while shouting ¡Levántense! thereby potentially setting-off a lifetime of heart complications and triggers; Nor would she yank the blanket from our bodies with the same speed and gusto as though she were trying to impress friends at a party by yanking the cloth from the table without disturbing the dinnerware.

No. My mother would simply turn on the TV, then the lights, then raise the volume to a moderate level, which sent a subtle nudge to our brains to gently wrap up our dream sequence. If after a few minutes (which was most often the case), she didn't hear the sound of steel straining as my brothers, sister, and I shifted from within any of our beds held in the two metal bunk beds we shared (this sentence lacks clarity it is a run on and this semi colon doesn't belong here); she would return to the bedroom and firmly caress our arms or legs until she saw that we were awake. She would repeat this until our groggy, half-asleep bodies got up one-by-one to make their ways to the bathroom to get ready.

My older brother Lemy, who was 13 years old at the time, was pretty much autonomous in terms of readying himself to go to his junior high school, which was only five streets away from our apartment. As such, my mother's morning routine was primarily focused toward her younger children: Me, 9 years old (in the fourth grade), my sister, Rosabelis, 5 years old (first grade), and my younger brother, Angel, 4 years old (kindergarten).

She was a single mother of four, with a considerable language barrier at the time, no transferable academic accreditation from her home country, and a lack of familial and/or professional support. Our mother, like many others with a similar narrative, depended on food stamps (*cupones)* and whatever other government assistance programs she was eligible for, which helped supplement this or that particular expense and kept our asses above water.

The *cupones* kept our refrigerator modestly stocked with essentials. Milk, eggs, bread, and certain cereal brands? Yes. Jarol secretly tossing a pack of Oreos into the grocery cart and hoping that my mother would pay the $3.25 for the goddamn cookies? No. Whatever financial assistance program she was eligible for, she would use wisely and proactively. Our mother would supplement all leftover expenses by working as a "beauty consultant" for Mary Kay, a cosmetics and beauty supply company that operated by having its distributors (beauty consultants) work through a multi-level marketing model. It was, in essence, a lipstick and mascara pyramid scheme. This was our mother's occupational source of income.

Whatever financial prospects our mother did have while working for Mary Kay was short-lived. This was not due to a lack of salesmanship skills or interest. It started with our mother receiving a series of pages to her beeper from our elementary school. Either Angel had gotten into it with a classmate or instructor or I was being disruptive in class. These phone calls reasonably intererfered with my mothers ability to work in one peace.

The year 1999 came. We moved from 189th street to 158th street as I entered the fifth grade. Angel had been unfairly placed in the Special Education system, which I believe bruised his self-esteem and spirit of motivation. My older brother, Lemy, would grow into a latent pathological resentment towards my mother.

I envy my mother's patience. I've never met someone who holds space for people in the genuine manner that she does. She's the type that listens to listen and only offers feedback if you ask for it. Her unyielding resilience, forged from her own upbringing and life on the island, accompanied her to this new land. Mostly though, I admire our mother's unwavering optimism. It is her voice that echoes through the chasms of my being when parts of life's journey feel uncertain and unjust. "Todo está bien. Y todo va salir bien."—*All is well. All will be well.* Her hugs alone have the power to temporarily repel doubt and fear. She had conditioned us not to see the struggle. She balanced our lives as best she could, with what little she had, so that we may never covet another, nor see ourselves superior to another. If ever she had to borrow money from a friend in order to put food in the fridge, we never saw it;
And so I was caught off guard when meeting the likes of my college friend, Mo, whose parents limited his expenditures to only $800/week; Or my high school friend, Jaime, whose mother had to pull her out of weekend equestrian classes on the Upper West Side in order to save on expenses after her divorce; Or my high school friends, twins Jake and Ian. Like me, Jake and Ian grew up in New York City. Unlike me, they were white, and alternated every week between living at their mother's apartment in Downtown Brooklyn and their father's high-rise apartment in Tribeca. These friendships started to make me question class, wealth, and where my family fell on the hierarchy.

One hot June afternoon, classes let out early. Ian decided to come uptown with our friend Matthew, a fellow classmate and friend. Like me, Matthew is brown. He has a mixed background and was adopted by a kind and lovely Welsh teacher when he was an infant. Unlike me, Matt had been raised in the East Village, with private Cello lessons after school since the age of seven. To this day, Matthew can lull a waterfall to sleep with his instrument. We arrived at my family's apartment on 158th street. "*Bendición, mami,*" I say to my mother as I kiss her on the cheek. My friends follow me into the kitchen. I introduce them to my mom and we make our way to the living room to turn on the PlayStation.

44

Shortly thereafter, mom begins to fry up some tostones with salami (Because when you're Dominican, it's indecent to bring a first-time guest over, and not offer them something to eat and/or drink. It's seen as inhospitable, and rude.). I've always known this. I learned the hard way that this wasn't an across-the-board ideology in other cultures. Just the day prior, the twins, Matt, and I played basketball in the park across the street from their father's apartment. Back at the apartment, we laughed and chatted with their dad as we sat around the kitchen island. He prepared turkey sandwiches just for him and his sons. To my great brown-skin surprise, it appeared that having excess did not automatically program you to share. By contrast, I began to understand that having little makes you appreciate what little you have. That, by default, connects you to the idea that another might be in need as well.

I walk back into our living room, plates in hand. I place the meals on the table. Knowing better than to eat the already delicious meal as is, I go back to the kitchen to get the ketchup (this sentiment is confusing to me because why would you need to get ketchup for something that you also claim is good as is. Your reader may not understand the connection. You can make the same point in less words). I open the refrigerator door and frown when I see how violently squeezed the bottle was; nothing left but the ketchup precum. I shake the bottle to see if anything would shift— *nada*. I re-entered the kitchen with such purpose that I hadn't seen mom sitting on the little red chair in the corner; the same red chair, which has followed our family since we lived on 189th street. My mother, the master of rainchecks and supermarket deals within the Tri-State area, would certainly have a replacement bottle somewhere, right? I asked, "Ma, y el kachú?" Mami plops down in the chair with her face hidden in her palms, and for the first time in my life, I see it. It would be years before I would see it again.

At this moment, I understand that my mother is not ashamed or disappointed that there's no ketchup in the house. Rather, she is ashamed that I might be able to see that the only reason my friends and I are eating tostones and salami is because that's all that there was to make. She still hadn't fed my siblings, who hadn't arrived home yet. She is thinking of what to make for her kids, or if she can borrow $15 from the *vecina* to maybe order *chinitos* or something.

Mami doesn't scold me. She doesn't seem upset or anything. That's not what my mom does. It's never been something she does.

Our mother merely takes a deep breath, pulls her hands away from her face, and with that gentle smile, which we've come to identify her by, through visibly glistening, tear-stricken eyes she simply replies, "¿Tú estás seguro mi hijo?"

Café con leche - Roberto Germán

Ah! The taste of café con leche
acculturation of coffee and milk
island fresh idea imported to The States
mixing, blending
forming one from two
holding onto old traditions
while establishing customs that are new
Azúcar
Acculturation of coffee and milk
drawing both to a compromise
steam rise
let your scent resurrect from jarros
remain lleno de color y vida
don't let the culture of café assimilate
to the point that you only drink leche
Sabor
Bebiendo despacio
mientras tanto entregándome pedazos de casabe
save these pieces of ancestry
y mándame una copia
de café con leche

Un Verano en Nueva York - Caroline Saldaña

"Un refresco y papita Lays," I told the azafata
who accompanied me on my 12-teen summer trip to La
República Dominicana.

Every summer, mami would send me on a plane so that she
could pick up extra shifts at Caridad and open the *salón* til' late.

I would look out the window, nostalgic
because I really wished to be home on the block
opening la pompa, getting soaked and eating ices with my friends.

I wanted so desperately to be a part of their back to school summer
stories; see, mami worked so hard
she never wanted me to miss out on my summers
so she found it best to send me to El Cibao with Mamá.

One summer in Moca, tío Mello touched my
shoulder a little too rough.

Next summer, he pulled my skirt up just a little,
enough to fulfill his desires to see my frail legs and fat
deprived thighs swing from the *mecedora* in mamá's *galería*.

I was always afraid to speak up and when I did, all I got was
"Eso no es nada muchacha del diablo. Ese es tu tío."

Seventh grade summer came and I decided to purposely fail
my math class so that I could be enrolled in summer school.

See, summer school prevented me from taking the 4 hour plane ride to
Santiago this summer.

Mami was furious that I failed
but this summer I refused to let
Tío Mello fulfilled his perverted fantasies.

I didn't get to spend my days in the salon helping *mami* do *rolos* or
buying 10 cent ices in the bodega on Valentine Avenue.

NI DE AQUÍ, NI DE ALLÁ

I didn't get to jump double dutch or
get in the pump with my best friends
and in case you were wondering,
no, I didn't get to be a part of my friends summer stories.

Instead, I spent my summer days in Ms. Hyman's class
and my nights *arrodillada*, praying to God that my
mother wouldn't disown me.

One night that summer, Mamá called and gave us the news that Tío
Mello had had a heart attack and left us.

I didn't know if there was a God at that age, or how he worked, but I
knew that he didn't like ugly.
I knew that if I prayed hard enough for my suffering to end, he would
come through.

Hunger: Things I Learned from Papi - Ser Alida

in total we were 4.
well, 5—papi negó a Daniel.

pero son igualitos,
aunque Daniel carga en los ojos
la vergüenza que papi no tuvo.

lo dejó en *Lo' Mina*
lamiéndose los sueños,
dodging falling bullets,
skipping meals,
jealous of his kin—waiting
behind the walls of Papi's denial.

Daniel wouldn't know it,
but we all inherited papi's absence equally.
even at the head of our dining table,
donde papi nunca nos miró a los ojos,
donde no aprendimos a perdonarlo.

NI DE AQUÍ, NI DE ALLÁ

Searching for Home- Aila Shai Castane

It's unusually warm for an early winter morning. The sun is shining from the giant windows overlooking the airplane tarmac. I notice people rushing to their gate with their heavy coats and winter scarves. I am dressed in thin jeans, lavender and indigo-colored New Balance sneakers, and a single layer long-sleeve shirt. Sweat begins to form on my forehead as the room gets more and more crowded. I sit in the Ft. Lauderdale airport, 22 years old, with my maletas on the floor next to my hard, plastic seat. I'm awaiting my flight to Holguin, Cuba. I am alone— surrounded by families who seem to have been here before. A familiar feeling creeps under my skin.

Outsider. Wanderer. Visitor.

Pero, ¿tú ta loca? ¿Pa' donde té te vas? Siempre inventando. I remind myself that this is bigger than me. This trip. This journey. This pilgrimage. Perhaps that will ease the nerves. I sit still, but my mind is racing—as if my insides are moving fast but the world around me is moving slow. *Can anybody see me right now?*

I've been communicating with my father's cousin via email for a year now and, finally, I am on my way to discover and connect with a hidden piece of myself. What a wild treasure hunt Spirit was sending me on. I am eager to meet my family for the first time and they are eager to meet me too. They keep asking when I plan to visit. Our emails grow more and more constant. My cousin tells me all about our lineage—how we originally come from the Congo region of Africa, which family members are still alive, which ones have passed, and the children that survive them. This is the power of oral history. Yet here I am, on my first solo trip abroad, nervous. It doesn't occur to me that I might get lost, kidnapped, robbed, or stranded without a working phone, or any of the countless horrors any normal human being would be worried about. No. I am afraid of something else. I am afraid I won't find what I am searching for.

Home never felt like home long enough for me to feel comfortable. At the time, home was Richmond, Virginia, where I was finishing up my last semester of undergrad. My time there was temporary. My parents reside in Virginia Beach, where they await their negrita bella becoming the first to earn a degree and even there I feel displaced. An Afro-Latina born in Washington Heights and raised in the suburbs? Yeah, talk about an identity crisis. If I didn't understand who I was, my white classmates that dominated the halls of my gifted K-12 education sure as hell didn't either. I was, and still am, always itching to leave. I am always in search of something. I can't quite put my finger on it. Always trying to connect the dots to the puzzle that is my existence. Independence is what some people call it—my knack for wandering off by myself, be it physically across streets, cities, subway stops, state lines, or oceans; or spiritually, with an incense stick, palos music, and a notebook filled with questions for the spiritual realm that I didn't quite know how to ask. Do my ancestors even understand English? I sometimes think my misfortunes are a result of the language barrier in my prayers. Maybe that's why I became a dancer. In all of these places, I go searching; And in all of these places, my body is a vessel for transportation on my journey.

I arrive in Cuba. As I walk out of the airport, I am met with a series of faces of varying hues. My eyes land on the dark one. His features, somewhat similar to my father's, are familiar to me. He's holding a sign with my name written on it in all caps. AILA SHAI CASTANE. His eyes light up when they meet mine. He rushes to embrace me—all of me. How refreshing it is to feel seen.

However, I am overwhelmed as the day goes on. Everyone is excited to see me, meet me, and search for traces of my grandfather within me. I am afraid I don't measure up or meet their expectations. Am I too American? Is my Spanish too broken? Is my complexion too light? Is my hair too curly? Does my connection to my Dominican heritage overshadow my connection to them? Am I relatable? Do they love me? Do they feel me? Do they see me? I sit on the floral-patterned couch, watching the small living room fill up with family members and people I didn't even know existed. Everyone converses with each other with ease. *This is home for them.* I thought it would be home for me too, but I feel foreign, like I don't belong. I am a visitor, a spectator. I am not from here. I am not of here.

I am handed a ziplock bag. Inside are pictures and worn letters, pieces of my family's history, including my great grandfather's identification card, pictures of his wife and their children. I had struck gold. Then I came across a picture of me. *How long have they known about me?* I pause and study my photo harder. We don't give enough credit to our younger selves, content with our realities and the homes that we know. At what point do we grow up wanting more?

As the night falls and my family members head back to their homes, the living room is suddenly empty. My cousin and my aunt, who own the home that I am staying in, leave briefly to walk another cousin to their home. It's just me, the floral-patterned couch, and the television. My family lives in el campo so they don't have cable. USB flash drives with the latest tunes and music videos are a hot commodity around here. I use the remote control and flip through a bachata playlist. I land on an older Aventura music video - *Tell My Why.*

Wow, what a throwback. I always loved this song and the mix between Spanish and English; The duality. I listen to the lyrics, the guitar, and the melody.

> *I don't know what's going on with my baby*
> *Por qué ya no me quiere ver*
> *She doesn't want to talk to me*
> *She left one early morning without reasons*
> *Sin dejarme una cartita*
> *Or a clue where she might be at*
> *I don't think that I deserve what you have done*
> *I don't sleep and I don't eat esperando for your love*

Bachata was the first genre of music I fell in love with. I let Romeo's voice fill my body as I swayed in place. I think about the girl he is talking about. I start to feel for her. *Where did she go? What is she looking for?*

I imagine what she looks like, the girl he is crooning about. What stories live in her eyes? What about her heart? What narratives live in her body? Is she running away or running towards? As I think about her, my swaying grows bigger and bigger. I allow myself to take up space. I move from the middle of the room to the wall. Then to the other wall. Then to the corners, and soon my sways turn into steps - the "1-2-3-hip" movement of my body fills the room.

> *Cuándo volverás*
> *When will you come back*
> *Ay dime mami donde tú estarás*
> *When will you come back*
> *Cuándo volverás*
> *Dime morena ay dónde andarás*

Maybe she doesn't know where she is going. Maybe she just intuitively knows that it's time to move. Maybe she is in Santo Domingo. Maybe she fled to Cuba. Maybe she just wanted to dance, to be seen. To be. Maybe she is me. *Déjala.*

The rest of my trip is still a blur but I remember feeling out of place on more than one occasion.

Laments of an American-born Latina.

Laments of a colonized tongue.

Laments of a first-generation college student.

Laments of an Afro-Latina sitting on the border between here and there.

Is it possible to be homesick for a place I've never met?

Why do I long for a place I am not entirely sure exists? What is this sense of belonging that I desire so badly?

These questions lived in my mind for the remainder of my time in Cuba. I kept thinking about my body and how my skin, my bones, my veins make up the only home that remains constant. And while my skin may scar, my bones become brittle, and my blood sheds, my body remains a safe haven to house all of my stories and secrets. Mine is a body that grows and expands, changes and adapts, moves through time, space and geography.

> *I wanted this body to remember.*
> *I wanted this body to know that it was my home first.*

NI DE AQUÍ, NI DE ALLÁ

One week after my return to the United States, I decide to pay homage to this body. I leave campus and walk to the tattoo shop up the street. I show the white receptionist a picture of what I want and am met with a quizzical look.

> "I want the words 'Ni de aquí on my left foot and 'Ni de allá on my right"

A tattoo artist nearby hears me and starts laughing. I can't figure out what is so funny. He is Latino. Maybe he just doesn't get it because when people look at him, they just *know*. Or maybe he just knows who he is and the home he belongs to. His laughter is a reminder of my "otherness," which is the reasoning behind my tattoo. This body. This borderland body. Maybe I am not meant to be understood.

I pay the receptionist and wait for my turn. Rock music fills the room in stark contrast to the reggaeton and bachata I danced to just the week before, in Holguin.

My tattooist calls my name. "Ah-Lay-Uh?"

He butchers it of course. They always do. I walk behind the curtain, kick off my sandals, and hop on the bench.
I take a deep breath before the needle penetrates my skin. I remember how I felt amongst my family in the living room: *out of place*. I remember how I felt at the airport in Ft. Lauderdale: *lonely*. I remember how I felt in grade school as the only colored face in my class, *othered*.

The needle drags and the ink remains. The wound replaced with memory.

> *I remember.*
> *I remember.*
> *I remember.*

I think back to this trip often. At the time, I was reading Gloria Anzaldua's *Borderlands/La Frontera* for my Latina feminism class, during my last semester of undergrad. I can't help but realize the borders that exist in my own life; Too black; Not black enough; Too American; Not American enough; Too Latina; Not Latina enough. I can never fully step into one world. I can never fully experience my body in its entirety. One foot here and one foot there. I am not from any one place. I am from a million different places. I sit at the intersection of here, there, familiar, strange, Black, Latina, American, foreign, nigga, morena, negra, prieta, English, Spanish, Cuba, Dominican Republic, New York, Virginia, pelo bueno, pelo malo, light skin, dark skin, gringa…the list goes on.

Maybe home isn't a place. Maybe home isn't a physical destination that we try to reach. Maybe it's a mindset and a state of being. Maybe the only home we'll ever know is the body that we live in. My feet have taken me many places. My feet will continue to take me to many places—whether physically, to different locations or spiritually, through the high I feel when I dance. My feet elevate me. My spirit connects with those who are responsible for who I am today. My body is used as a vessel for our stories. When I dance, when I connect with the drums, when I am taken to a new place, I am home. My body, my spirit, my soul is home.

Ni de aquí. Ni de allá.
I am from everywhere.
And home is me. I am home.

Women from la línea-Sydney Valerio

to come from la línea in DR means to come
from the line & what they mean is the border
& border towns exist as the boundary drawn between
two countries that share an island full of syncretized
roots & families full of bodies constantly scanned by
one another constantly trafficked & generationally trapped in line & in
movement

women from la línea see their bodies with the same
laser focus men use & by the time they reach a
ripe state in adolescence naturally wide hips are questioned about when
they will carry a baby
by the time they hit 25 they better have a man &
a family plan or their agency & their currency runs dry like el río Yaquet
during summer months till winter & patronales arrive & bodies swell like
the river's bank

women from la línea include my young aunt who was introduced via a
line up of pictures to the husband who paid for her surgeries after giving
him two kids
& he first looked at her while sitting at a barber shop in the Bronx pic by
pic he said to my father

si ella ta buena
esa es la mía

women from la línea are said to be wild
said to be always in heat
always ready & Johnny Ventura wrote a
whole song entitled
Me Tiene Enredao about how the women from Castañuelas are difficult
in the daytime
& stick onto men in the nighttime
they are ingrates who then latch on like dog
fleas like dog fleas like fleas on dogs they latch on
& men twist onto them like snakes & Johnny Ventura
is an icon of merengue & that's what he had to say
about women from Castañuelas

he sang this when Mamá was in her 40s & Mamá had thirteen children -
nine were women- so when the eldest daughter decided to leave to NYC
I can see how Mamá supported that trip & tía never had children

in NYC, Mami was raised in Harlem at the height of the 70s & the
Dominican culture came to NYC too & lines of drugs I mean lines to the
clubs became part of their reality

as a woman in NYC Mami could be married to someone in DR for them
to get their papers & yes when I was sixteen like ritual Mami asked me
& still holds a grudge because I refused. She'll play it off like she
doesn't know what I'm talking about but I learned at that age how to
draw a line between my mother & me learned to create that generational
break of a cycle &

it's a twisted line
a boundary
between
mother
land and me
one that is necessary
for me & my
daughters
to untwist
& liberate
our lineage.

NI DE AQUÍ, NI DE ALLÁ

Are we a spill or are we a landslide? – Natasha Soto

In response to a DNA test someone gifted to me.

I learned that my ancestors had floated like seeds on the winds of:
the original sin of avarice, then coercion, then, perhaps, an orphaned
necessity.

I had a fuzzy picture (word choice) that we were a mix of Spanish,
African, and indigenous Americans because of a painful tale I knew by
heart.

We spoke Spanish at home and my parents had come from Latin
America, after all.

My parent's love story played out in my DNA. One parent was from the
Dominican Republic, the other from Ecuador; bound together by the
desire to start something new someplace else.

I wanted to know what was gained along the way. Maybe this test could
show me.

The countries and first nations that appeared seemed to span the whole
world.

That my ancestors were intrepid didn't shock me. To participate in this
world is to move through it.

But still, wouldn't it be nice to stay put? To plant a garden? To tend to it?
(Today, I am world-weary and tired.)

When looked at on a continuous timeline, where each person born picks
up where their ancestor left off, people are just movement. Sometimes
it's a spill, sometimes a mudslide. We are always in transit for the next
safe place or next best thing, melting and reshaping boundaries in their
(who is "their"?) wake.

La novia del Atlántico - Gisselle Belia

Un himno para sí sola,
Ella ya no es la misma,
pero aún guarda su mismo esplendor,
nadie la puede mal versar.

Juguetona, no se logra vislumbrar nada más que no sea su vestido azul
turquesa,
y el pañuelo blanco que a lo lejos casi la toca.
Se mezcla contigo y te hace sentir que perteneces.
Ella te espera y se desploma con caricias a veces inmóviles pero vivas.

Tan lejos de casa
no tienes patria.
A veces el encono de verte en aquel lugar,
Te das cuenta que ya no te posee,
Se cambia el vestido, no sonríe igual, es fría.

Quiero sentirte y me pierdo en la traducción de mis recuerdos.
No comprendo, eres la misma pero diferente,
para ellos eres amor de verano y para mí la cálida novia del Atlántico.

Te vas tan rápido entre tus montañas.
No te consumo, me consumes a mí,
y vivo al recordar que me atrapas y no me dejas escapar de ti.

La luna parece tuya cuando cae sobre ti como la sinfonía de un
merengue.
No hay mucho que ver en la oscuridad de este letargo sin fin,
y todo que añorar hasta que regrese a ti.

Morado- Albert García

The almond tree, taller than any building I've seen in New York cloaks the house from the sun's laser beam rays. As soon as the truck stops, Max and I jump out and start taking the luggage out from the back. The little rocks covering every inch of the yard could be felt through the soles of my all white Nike sneakers. Max is already trying to knock the dust off of his pair from the jump we made. Back home, keeping white Nikes clean is all people care about. Now that he has a pair, he's reaching down every few steps to check for scuffs or marks. I don't really care for mine except for the way they protect me from these sharp ass rocks. Behind my grandma, who's thanking God for our arrival, is a barefoot girl walking over to us.

She was watering the plants that surround the house and seemed to have forgotten her sandals in the excitement of our arrival. She came straight towards me and said, "Bienvenido, mi nombre es Jessica," As if these rocks were the softest carpet. Her mouth played Spanish, smooth like jazz. Her thick hair definitely resembled that of the Sánchez family. Her soft afro was tied up in a bun, but her light green eyes seemed out of place. They were probably from her mother's side. Before I could say hi, Max yells over the clucks coming from the chicken coop, "Prima, ¡ni cuanto tiempo!" He thinks he's a full dominicano just because he came with Mami for three days a couple years ago, when our great-grandmother died. Max gives Jessica a huge hug before they start to catch up. Grandma comes over to me and gives me a kiss on the cheek. She says how happy she is to see me before turning back to help my mom with her bag.

After I finish unpacking weeks worth of clothes, I come out to the porch and sit on the rocking chairs where Max and Jessica have been talking the entire time. It was starting to get dark out and I hadn't gotten a single word in on the conversation because of their constant back and forth. The rhythm they have is weird(choose a more accurate adjective to describe this). How could she connect with my brother better than I can? The better question is, how could I be jealous of it? The hot winds turned into slow breezes, brushing between the leaves of the campo and muffling the sounds of the motorcycles passing through our street. Jessica told us about a club, not too far from the house, where we could go this weekend after Max kept insisting on doing something crazy. I stood to get their attention.

"Did you guys forget about Grandma, Mami, and Uncle Miguel? One of them will definitely find out."

Jessica responded to me, "My Dad can come with us. He won't say anything, trust me. Just don't drink too much."

Max let out the ugliest laugh I've ever heard. "You see, hermanito, nothing to worry about."

He gets up from his chair and pulls Jessica to dance, while humming a bachata I can't put my finger on. They're the same height even though she doesn't have any shoes on.

"I know you're not going to dance in the club like that."
Before I finish my sentence, she replies, "Of course not, I can move even better in my heels."

Max loses his footing from the laughter before quickly finding it and smiling like nothing happened. They continue to dance while I walk to the store for a soda. From across the street, I could hear the guys in the store talking. They go back and forth over beers as they sat on one-hundred-pound sacks of rice, about the Americanos who just came from Nueva Yol. Two of them don't look over thirty, but as I get closer, their wrinkled faces and dull skin confuses me. The one behind the counter smiles, revealing a gold tooth in his mouth that sparkles through the dusk (great description).

Before I walk in, one of them says in Spanish, "Solo necesita escuchar cómo hablan español para saber que son realmente dominicanos. Si eso no ayuda, pregúntele cuánto le gusta el mangú. Y si no comen plátano de cena cinco veces a la semana, llévelo a un lado y pídale que bailen bachata. Sabrás por como se mueven."

The laughs erupt from their beer-filled bellies, while I walk in and ask for my soda. Their remarks of what it means to be Dominican, such as knowing how to speak Spanish a certain way, how much and how often you're supposed to eat plantain a week, and knowing how to dance bachata don't surprise me. Maybe it's my bad Spanish or maybe my clothes. These white Nikes sure do stand out with the campo as its backdrop. I feel like I don't belong, even though we all look alike. Back in New York, people who look alike usually stick together, and among my Hispanic friends in Washington Heights, I was the most Dominican. These guys must've been drinking all day. They can't even recognize one of their own. I let out a fake laugh and make my way back to the house.

Max and I watch the highlights on ESPN for a couple of minutes before I get bored and decide to go to bed. Aside from the Sánchez hair, the only thing we have in common is our flan looking skin. Not at the top, where it's nice and glossy brown, that's more like Jessica's complexion. Max and I are like the middle, right when the caramel is sliding down. Jessica is already snoring in the next room, but I can barely hear her after turing the fan on. I slide under the bed net and close my eyes, while the crickets outside and the light drizzle of rain on the zinc roof lullaby me to sleep.

-

The next day goes by quickly. Max sits in front of the colmado with the guys from the day before, drinking from a small bottle of Brugal blanco and playing dominoes. When I pass by, they seem to be having fun, but as time goes by, they grow nastier. Sweat stains build around their armpits. They can't seem to be able to stand up straight without taking their three amazing bachata steps for balance. I could hear them from down the road. Clinking his bottles together, one of the guys proudly announces, "¡Máximo es un verdadero dominicano!"

That night, Jessica and I are ready and waiting for Max in the car with Uncle Miguel. She's wearing a black dress and the heels she mentioned a few days ago. Her dad is wearing a dress shirt, with the top three buttons undone, showing his thin gold chain. He's on the phone with a woman, telling her he'll be there soon. I have on the only dressy shirt I brought here, a short sleeve satin purple shirt. Max storms into the truck, smelling like a Macy's perfume counter. We each roll down our windows to breathe. He wears a super tight white polo that shows the muscles he had been working on for the trip.

"Damnnn bro, did you shower in cologne?"

He smirks, "Not for you, it's for the ladies."

Jessica rolls her eyes, "Let's go, Papi, before we pass out in here."

Uncle Miguel, eager to go, steps on the gas. The Caribbean breeze flushes Max's stench out of the car. *La Jungla* hangs over the entrance in lime green lettering, with plastic vines and leaves draped over it. The bouncer gives Uncle Miguel a firm handshake. As the rest of us walk in, they stay behind us. He comes in after a few seconds to show us our table, a bucket of beers as our centerpiece.

Uncle Miguel says, "Alright, I'll be at the bar, have fun," taking off while he's still talking.

Max opens our beers while following the song's beat with his shoulders, and passes them to us before drinking his own. Sweaty bodies are in all directions, caused by hips rolling against pelvises in a populated room. The air's heavy from hookah smoke, making it a hundred times hotter. Jessica points out her friends from college to us and waves them over. A few songs play, but I don't say a word except for the initial, "Hola, my name is Videl."

Jessica tells her friends, "These are my cousins from New York. They're only here for a few more days."

Both girls' eyes light up and so does Max's when he notices their rising interest. One of Jessica's friends keeps looking at me whenever she takes a sip from her straw. I think she said her name was Paola. She has a light birthmark, the shape of a limoncillo, right above her left breast. She tries to cover it by bringing all of her brown hair forward to her left side. I look away, trying to keep my cool. Hopefully she doesn't notice the sweat stains under my arms. She dances her way around the table and towards me while I continue my two-step. After two songs, she

64

grabs my shoulder down and I lean in. She's just inches from my ear but I can barely hear her. She smacks her lips together, emitting sprinkles of cold saliva on my neck. She says, "I love this song." It looks like the group of girls on the other side of the club also favor this old-school bachata. They scream in sequence like a flock of birds, maneuvering past the guys who have been burning holes through their skin tight dresses. Paola pulls me onto the crowded dance floor. When I look back, Max is pushing up behind me with the other girl. His smile almost reaches the earrings Mami nearly ripped off of me last summer.

He flows from one end of the dancefloor to the other, spinning and twirling with his partner. I remain grounded in the corner closest to our table, dancing with Paola. My steps feel like cinder blocks compared to the grace coming from her silver heels. I look down at them, trying to keep up.

She looks up at me. "You don't know how to dance?"
"No, not really."
"That's cute," she says, trying to make the situation less awkward.

I say, "Thanks," and accidentally brush all of her hair towards her back, revealing her birthmark. She continues dancing but steps back to bring her hair forward again.

I say amidst the guitar solo blasting from the speakers, "No, it's cute. Don't be ashamed."

She smiles and I spin her around. On our way back to the table, Jessica gives me the eye when we return. "You two are having a lot of fun," she says, sarcastically with a smirk on her face. I overhear the people next to us make fun of my dancing and calling me a gringo, but I ignore it. Uncle Miguel and his date come over to party with us and everyone dances with one another for a few hours.

Max, who is now on the couch, drinks water by the gallon, trying to sober up before returning to the house. Jessica is with her friend on the dancefloor and Uncle Miguel is smooth talking his date by the exit. Paola bobbles over to me and leans on my chest. She mumbles about how amazing the night was before stretching her neck and puckering her lips in an attempt to kiss me. I let her kiss me on the cheek. Her eyebrows fully meet, expressing confusion. I tell her how much fun I had dancing. It's even harder to not kiss her after feeling those soft lips on my cheek. I know for certain they are sweet, like the cotton candy colored gloss painted on her lips; but I've heard what girls think of guys who come from New York. I'm definitely not turning into the viejos from the block, who only come to the island to be with a few girls to feed their egos and drain their pockets.

Paola hugs me, and for a second I think of how things would be if we ever got into a serious relationship—but I know it'll never really work.

"Nunca te avergüences de nada," I tell her while brushing her hair back. She smiles, causing her lip gloss to shine through the night club's thick foggy air. "Podemos mantenernos en contacto," she says while handing me her number with a tiny heart drawn on it. I slide the piece of paper in my pocket and kiss her. It was as soft as I'd imagined, only better. She hugs me tighter. Uncle Miguel calls out, "Vámonos," and we all say goodbye. Paola's eyes begged for me not to go, but they relaxed when I told her I'd call. She laughed as I walked away, saying "Le diré a tu prima que te busque si no llamas." I laughed because I'd heard how tough she can be from Max, and so having Jessica look for me is the last thing I'd want. "Confía en mí" was the last thing I told her.

Uncle Miguel drops(you have to maintain the same tense throughout. Switching back and forth while keeping the setting/time frame the same is confusing for your reader) off his date not too far from the house. We pull into the patio around 1 a.m. nice and slow, making sure not to wake anyone up. Jessica and I walk Max into the house so he can go to bed. Uncle Miguel walks to his room, whispering into the phone, probably to his date or some other woman. Jessica goes to her room and I sit at the edge of my bed. The fan blows on my sweaty shirt as it surveils (wrong word choice) the room side to side.

The dark room, separated by a beam of blue moonlight, creates two worlds under the same roof. My purple button-up glistens like wet grapes as I pass the beam. I feel my way towards the front door. The door creaks open as I pull on it, allowing light into the bleak living room. Until now, I hadn't noticed how bright the night was. I could see the outhouse's slouch perfectly by the pickup truck. The stars were scattered all over the sky, like God's freckles if he had a face, making me feel small in the world. This past week here in Dominican Republic was not what I thought it would be. I thought this was going to be a homecoming experience. In New York, I only felt comfortable around the black and hispanic people from my neighborhood. I would rush to take the train uptown after classes, running away from the subtle looks that implied that I didn't belong. The one train would calm the anxiety that crawled up my back. The smell of pastelitos cooking in the boiling oil of a street cart in Washington Heights helped relax me. I believed that coming to the Dominican Republic for the first time would feel as though Washington Heights was not just a neighborhood, but rather a whole country, with the smell of crispy pastelitos everywhere. Instead, I stick out here as much as I do around the white people of midtown New York. If I had to explain how it feels to be a stranger on my own land, I would say it's like hugging a ghost; you open your arms for the warmest embrace, but as you pass through the figure, coldness seeps into your bones, leaving you aching and craving inclusion.

"Should I have kissed her?" I sigh while kicking the pebbles on the ground. The bushes feel like they contain predators, staring through its dense branches.

"Max would've, and probably any other real Dominican." I run my fingers on my lips as I feel the kiss fade away.

The cricket's flute-like symphony deepens with bass and speeds up. I come back inside before anyone wakes up to realize I'm not in bed. I lay awake realizing the reality of the two worlds I live in. I whisper to my pillow, "It was my choice not anyone else's."

This purple shirt is a sore thumb no matter where it goes. It's a unique combination of the primary colors blue and red. Tonight, sadness tried to choose me for its nourishment, but I evaded it. I belong neither here nor there. I reside wherever my heart feels home.

Confessions of Un Dominicano - Enmanuel Cabreja

The iron fist led me to fear you
not respect you.
I was afraid to come to you
with my problems.
I was afraid to tell you the truth.
Correazos made me a coward.
They corroded my trust.
Eroded my self-esteem.
It took years to rebuild.
To revive.
To be brave.
To confide.
To find confidence
but what hurt me most,
more than the physical pain,
was that when I cried,
you'd hit me harder,
and I learned
I couldn't cry.
I shouldn't feel.
It was a sort of psychological torture.
I became a barrel
of unresolved emotions;
a barrel of explosives.

I blew up more times than I should have.
Used my iron fists when I shouldn't have.
I was hurtful when I could have walked away.
And it took a lot of work to get to this place;
where I can write this without feelings getting in the way.

Not because you beat them out of me,
but because I learned discipline.
Because I gave myself validation.
Because I owned my mistakes
and made amends
with those I gave my pain to.
Because I learned to forgive you.

NI DE AQUÍ, NI DE ALLÁ

Because I learned to love in healthy ways.
Because I learned to feel again
and it feels amazing.
And for you,
I feel sad.
Sad because you loved
the way you were taught,
and that must have been
fo you,
because when I look at you,
I see years of pent up quiet rage;
decades in barrels waiting to blow up.

I pray for you;
that you find peace,
discipline,
validation.
I hope you make amends
with those you gave
your frustrations to.
I hope you forgive your iron fist.
The correazos.
The cocotazos.
Learn to love,
to feel again.
before it's too late.

Sin etiquetas- Roxana Calderón

Ya que estamos tan abiertos, me voy a permitir viajar al pasado y abrir puertas que, aunque ya cerradas, fueron parte fundamental de mi desarrollo.

Ese vaivén entre Santo Domingo y Estados Unidos casi me deja loca. Se obtiene mucho, pero también se pierde. En ese proceso de ir y venir casi me pierdo a mí misma o lo que pensaba que era; perdí el hilo con amistades, lazos familiares, se disminuyó mi patriotismo y entre otras cosas perdí la conexión que llevaba con mi isla.

Yo nací en Brooklyn, pero desde que tenía un año de edad residí en República Dominicana. A los diez años mami y yo tomamos la decisión de que yo regresara a Nueva York a vivir con una tía para aprender inglés y conocer otros horizontes. No abundaré mucho en el tema, pero, aunque esos dos años fueron inolvidables, también sufrí un paquetón. El que quiera saber con más detalles que escuche la canción "Hasta que te conocí" de Juan Gabriel.

A esa edad comprobé que el que no tiene algo no lo puede ofrecer. Aunque económicamente nunca me faltó nada, me di cuenta que la ciudad de Nueva York no era lo mío. Conocí lo que era el *bullying*, la falta de cariño, la anorexia y la bulimia, el apoyo de personas que no eran de mi familia, el desprendimiento emocional hacia mi madre, la lejanía de mi padre, la incertidumbre de porque los dominicanos de mi isla bella eran diferentes a los dominicanos de la gran manzana, y el sonido de una voz subconsciente que se repetía en mi cerebro diciéndome "Aquí no perteneces".

NI DE AQUÍ, NI DE ALLÁ

Me "mudaron" de regreso a Santo Domingo, para completar el 1ro de bachillerato, porque me estaba "perdiendo". Durante mis primeros meses de clases en el nuevo colegio, mientras tomaba notas en mi cuaderno, escuché una conversación que tenían mis compañeros acerca de algo que hice, y pude escuchar como juzgaban mis actos por cosas a las cuales a mi entender eran normales, porque en Estados Unidos lo eran y yo venía de allá.

Mientras se me aguaban los ojos, empecé a escribir porque no me atreví a confrontarlos, y en mis líneas expresaba mi incomodidad al sentir que no encajaba en el lugar que estaba supuesto a moldear mi educación. Siempre fui la extraña, "la loca de familia disfuncional" que hacía o decía cosas que estaban fuera de lugar. Yo siempre fui muy abierta y eso de guardar las apariencias no se me daba bien. En ese colegio duré 3 años, y fueron los mejores de mi vida porque esta desencajada aprendió a moldearse de acuerdo al hábitat donde se encontraba. Lo que hice fue aprender a diferenciar lo que era bueno y positivo para mi progreso personal y soltar lo que me hiciese daño. Se lee muy bonito, pero no fue fácil, porque en el transcurso de esa etapa de mi vida también buscaba conocer quién era. Estaba en plena adolescencia, y a causa de la separación entre mi madre y yo, mientras vivía en Estados Unidos, me encontraba en la lucha de reconectar con la mujer que era mi madre, pero que a causa de la distancia yo solo veía como mi progenitora. Durante ese tiempo, en mi familia hubo drásticos cambios económicos, así que todo se sentía más fuerte.

Viví 3 años en un país que en mi infancia me llegó a abrazar con el alma, pero que al regresar me hizo sentir extraña, porque ya era lo suficientemente grande para entender y ser víctima directa e indirecta de sus reglas sociales, su doble moral, sus expectativas, su carencia de expansión mental y sus límites de aceptación.

A los 16 años regresé a la ciudad de Nueva York y cuando entré a la secundaria para terminar el 4to de bachillerato el nuevo cambio casi me fríe las neuronas. A pesar de que siempre era muy amistosa, y tenía muchos compañeros, siempre me sentía en el aire e irregular, así como cuando vivía en Santo Domingo. No podía profundizar con nadie porque no teníamos cosas en común. A mis 16 años de edad mis mejores amigos eran los maestros de la escuela y mi directora, aunque tiempo después encontré unos chicos que me salvaron la vida. Como siempre estaba sola y en mi mundo, mi tía me envió a un psicólogo. Yo pensaba que el psicólogo lo necesitaba para poder lidiar con ella, pero no. El psicólogo me puso como reto conocer a una persona diferente todas las semanas, y para mí eso fue casi imposible porque yo rehusaba sentarme a hablar con alguien de cosas banales y sin importancia. Yo quería hablar de Paulo Coelho y Unamuno, visitar museos de arte, conocer un restaurante nuevo, ir al teatro y hablar de filosofía. Nuevamente pasó por mí esa sensación maquiavélica de no pertenecer a ninguna parte. Me sentía como un yoyo, pero yo era quien siempre decidía regresar a ver el sol colarse con el frío por los rascacielos.

Me fui dando cuenta que si quería hacer amistades de mi edad me iba a tocar ser un poco más flexible, y hacer lo mismo que hice cuando residía en Santo Domingo; explorar el hábitat nuevo, conocer sus habitantes y sus costumbres, pero nunca dejarme influenciar al punto de olvidarme de quien era, o de en quién me estaba convirtiendo.

Durante mi exploración por el "nuevo mundo" descubrí que bailar bachata no me quitaba la clase, tomarme una cerveza a pico 'e botella no me hacía menos elegante y no sentarme con las piernas cruzadas no me hacía menos femenina. Al igual que bailar típico, o no exponer en todos lados mi bandera, y gritar a los cuatro vientos de donde soy y defender a todo pulmón la afro-latinidad no hacía más dominicana. Viajando de un lado al otro me di cuenta que el orgullo y el patriotismo se llevan en el corazón, y esto hace que tu cultura se transmita a través de ti sin necesidad de hacer mucho alboroto.

Aunque en Nueva York me vi rodeada de muchos dominicanos, con ellos fui capaz de aprender cosas que no me enseñaron los dominicanos de la República. La oportunidad de haber examinado y observado dos mundos totalmente diferentes, me obsequió uno de los regalos más grandes de mi vida; la habilidad de no tener que sentir que debo de encajar donde quiera que voy.

No es necesario que me marquen o comparen. Yo sé quién soy y de dónde vengo. No pertenecer ni me da, ni me quita, aunque entiendo que es importante sentirse identificado con alguien o algo, pero también es importante identificarse con uno mismo y las cosas que van esculpiendo quien en verdad somos.

NI DE AQUÍ, NI DE ALLÁ

En el viaje de aquí para allá y viceversa, pude hacer mi propio rompecabezas y colocar las piezas de ambas culturas donde sentí que mejor se acomodaban y no donde las personas, la sociedad, o mi entorno exigiesen que fuesen.

En ese transcurso también pude darme cuenta de que a pesar de que decimos ser "un pueblo unido" no lo somos. Estamos divididos entre los de allá, los de aquí, los del por el mundo entero, los que son pero no hablan o escriben en español, los que disfrutan lo popular, los que prefieren las cosas un poco más altas y los que como yo simplemente son, porque no encajamos en ningunas de nuestras dos patrias.

Para los de allá somos muy abiertos, y para los de aquí somos un producto al que se le puede dar buen uso dependiendo donde se nos ponga.

Se lee fácil, pero esta situación de evolución fue mucho más difícil que la primera, porque, aunque yo estuviese distante, mami siempre estuvo cerca, y durante la segunda exploración me faltó mucho amor. Las personas hablamos y juzgamos, y desde que detectamos que una persona no corresponde a nuestro patrón la tachamos, pero nunca analizamos los cambios que esta persona pudo, o puede estar atravesando. Hacemos referencia a tipos de frases como "mira, a ese se le ve que está recién salido del barco" pero no pensamos en lo que esa persona dejó del otro lado del mar. No pensamos que esa persona tenía una vida en otro lugar y ahora busca encontrarse un respiro a la vez. Solemos ser acogedores con nuestros actos, pero no con nuestra mente y hacemos que otro no se sienta ni de aquí, ni de allá.

Perplejidad - Wendy Mella Carreño

Todos llevamos ese algo por dentro;
the perplexity of finding out we don't belong
anywhere. Donde realmente pertenecemos,
somehow we depend on others to survive,
we rely on that second of empathy,
on that smile that asks, "¿tú tiene' un peso?"

Noches frías sentados en un McDonald's pensando:
¿por qué carajos cambiamos "oro por espejitos"?
Solo en el fondo de ese vaso de café amargo y frío
 vemos reflejados entre luces de neón una interrogante,
"What the fuck is the American Dream?"

Buscamos algún recibo en blanco que nos informe
la caducidad del tiempo. It doesn't matter that the expiration
date was yesterday.

Immigrant, foreigner, outcast, ¿cuál adjetivo te gusta más?
Numbness when you can't find your heart between all those
layers of clothing. When the express train is running local and you just
smile and remember que en la casa te espera
una sopa con aguacate.

Antes que me olvides- Yubany Checo

Mientras pego las losas de este piso, voy pensando en cómo me recuerdas. Si sabrás quien soy.
Ahora es más fácil para ti, pero más difícil para mí. Ya no tienes que tratar de adivinar si estoy bien o mal, si te miento o digo la verdad. Siempre supiste leer los tonos de mi voz, en especial aquellos falsos de felicidad con los que la envuelvo todavía.
Lula me dijo que ya no puedes salir sola. Después de los desastres en el baño, volviste a escapar y llegaste hasta el mercado público. Por suerte todos en el barrio saben que no estás bien. Prefiero recordarte frente al televisor viendo aquella novela mejicana, silbando cuando barrías las flores de jazmín que caían en el callejón. Yo silbo también, pero al inspector no le gusta, dice que eso distrae. Para mí que le molesta verme contento. Me sigue de cerca mientras llevo los dedos paralizados del frío y embarrados de esta vaina pastosa. ¡Joder!
Ya entiendo lo de aquella pregunta: ¿cuándo vienes mijo? Y yo siempre posponiendo una navidad tras otra. ¡Qué pena! Si lo hubiese sabido antes que tu memoria se acortaba... Espero que cuando vaya no te hayas olvidado de mí. Desde ahora te haré videollamadas, te lo prometo.
Recuerdo lo que me dijiste: «Solo nos tenemos a nosotros.» Por un momento pensé que también tenía a Ramonita. Pero por más explicaciones que le di, no quiso entender, se fue. No le hacía gracia que estuviera enviándote dinero. Quería que me olvidara de todo allá, inclusive de ti.
Ella tenía mucho yéndose y no me había dado cuenta. Ahora que lo pienso mejor, se fue por partes. Primero se llevó su cercanía, después cargó con todas sus palabras hasta que un día la vi salir hacia la fábrica y no regresó.

NI DE AQUÍ, NI DE ALLÁ

El inspector me vigila de cerca. Las losas deben quedar derechitas, brillosas como culo de rana, así lo manda la ciudad. Repite tanto eso que ya odio esas palabras.

Muchos allá dirán « tanto estudiar para venir a pegar losas a este país.» Pero es así, aquí no es lo que te gusta sino lo que aparece. Si lo que aparece es lo que te gusta entonces es un *plus* como dicen los rubios. Si te pones a esperar entonces te lleva el tren. ¡Esos trenes! Todos abarrotados de gente a la hora pico. Cada quien mirando para otro lado, rehuyendo el contacto visual. No creo que te montes en uno. Tú eres demasiado observadora, conversadora. Y la nieve... esa vaina es difícil. Te traeré cuando me haga ciudadano para que la conozcas. Ya lo decidí. Sé que me ha tomado mucho pero no he tenido suerte. La nieve cae como copitos suaves, sin hacer ruido. Todo se torna blanco y después triste. No me gusta, pero por ti, ¿qué no haría?

Ahora sin Ramonita me rinde más el dinero. Así que abriré una cuenta en el banco, sacaré mi licencia, reportaré más impuestos; ya me explicaron el truco. ¡Qué pendejo fui!

Además, el inglés...tú sabes, los idiomas nunca se me dieron. Cuando vine aquí me inscribí en un instituto, pero a una maestra le cogió conmigo y no regresé. Entiendo mucho solo que respondo en español y a la gente aquí no le gusta. No me creerás si te digo que me da vergüenza hablarlo. Me siento raro. ¿Cómo explicártelo? Yo con vergüenza, parece un chiste.

Pensándolo bien, no aguantarías la soledad en el sótano. Entrar y salir como un lobo de su madriguera. No aguantarías dejar de mirar a las personas en el tren, con lo parlanchina que eres. Y así todos los días hasta que te mueres... Te cansarías de esta rutina: todo rápido, sin tiempo para hablar, para relajarte. El sueño cuesta.

Me preocupa tu memoria, está por tirar de la cuerda y apagarte. Lula me lo dijo con esa voz chillona que le sale cuando las cosas no están bien. Le agradezco. Es buena muchacha. Se ha hecho cargo de ti. Aún piensa que puedo quererla, pero no sé mamá, no sé.

Dicen que eso de la memoria es progresivo. Un día te quedas en blanco. El cerebro se te desconecta. Nadie sabe cuándo sucederá, pero vas para allá.

Creo que eso te vino de tanto sufrir. Es lo que te queda de tantos desarreglos. Nacer es un afán, pero vivir es el mayor de todos. Aún así quiero que vivas al menos como un pajarito frente a la escopeta del cazador. No te faltará medicina, te lo prometo.

NI DE AQUÍ, NI DE ALLÁ

Si me vieras lleno de polvo dirías —¡Pobre muchachito mío!— Pero prefiero esto que el hambre. Hambre sureña clavada como un cactus en mi estomago. Con la frente llena de surcos donde has ido metiendo las frustraciones, las preocupaciones, las oraciones por mí, para que nada me pase en este país.

Hoy el cielo está gris. Así se pone en invierno. Quisiera cambiártelo por los verdes y azules del mar. Tú sabes que lo llevamos por dentro. El mar nos llena. Somos navegantes, solo nos falta un poquito de viento para llegar y una tacita de café. ¡Eso sí!

Nos sentaremos a ver la tarde desde el balcón, mamá, antes que me olvides.

Bye.

Am I Latina?- Inés Rivera

You stress about a word because words
never come easy to you, because the voices

in your head say: Breathe. State it plainly.
Directly. Save face. Because your mouth

utters a word over and over again
before tasting the salt of it; then releasing it

to an ear, expert at catching its origin
or the way it drums inside you like home

or fear, or the sting of someone correcting
a word you thought you could really taste.

You navigate the space of belonging
and rejection, between and across:

¡Una dominicana en Cuba, hablando
Inglés, qué absurdo!

You ask: am I Latina if Spanish never comes
easy to me? If English is home—and guilt?

If your island is part fiction, part lowercase
history? An island of inherited memories?

Your tongue is evidence that your island
is not your island, but home.

The woman's voice rings: *¡Una dominicana*
En Cuba, hablando Inglés, qué absurdo!

Tell her your island is drawn from memories
and migrations across centuries. Your tongue

is as lush as orchids, beckoning for mercy,
and the rolling boleros your aunts sang.

NI DE AQUÍ, NI DE ALLÁ

Tell her, no, Spanish has never come
easy to you, never-the-less, your tongue,

its very curve, its rivers and birds, maps
a borderless home no language can pin.

Soy hija o lo fui- Pamela M. Balbuena de Gardós

Soy hija o lo fui, del mangú y el arroz con habichuela, del pescado frito de un domingo de playa, soy o fui, hija del sol que pica en la espalda y de la humedad que embriaga su aire.

El día que me fui de la tierra que me vio nacer, el alma se me partió en dos. Me invadía la emoción de la vida que iba a construir. Con solo diecinueve años todo era aún sencillo, sin ataduras y libre de obstáculos. Solo el ver a mi madre rota y a mi padre aguantando en el aeropuerto, un verano del 2005, me recordó el sacrificio de mi decisión; no las playas de arena blanca y aguas cálidas, ni su comida, ni su merengue pegadizo, ni siquiera su olor a isla sino ellos, mis padres, mi familia.

Daba por hecho que amigos iba hacer, por allí donde anduviese, un hogar iba a construir, allí donde fuese. Pero padres solo tendría unos en la vida, y se quedaban allí, plantados como palmeras a orillas de un mar de lágrimas.

Soy hija o lo fui del merengue y la bachata, del perico ripiado, de la güira, la maraca y la tambora.

Me fui con dos maletas a rebosar, un esposo agarrando mis manos y toda la cultura quisqueyana que podía agarrar en mi alma y corazón. España fue el primer país que me acogió. Mentiría si negara que mucho me gustó. Y es que tuve la suerte de que el amor llamó a mi puerta muy temprano, siendo suficiente motivo para dejar todo lo que conocía por lo que a su lado pudiera conocer. Y con él recorrí medio mundo; de la China a Londres, de Suecia a Japón y así, un sin fin de países, cada uno tan diferente a mí pero de aquellos viajes aprendí. Mil vivencias robaron mis pasos por esos lugares bellos y extraños.

Soy hija o lo fui del agua de coco, del frio frio, del jugo de caña y del refresco rojo, morado y naranja.

Un acento retocado y palabras robadas de otros mares es lo primero que se nota en mi hablar, para que otros se atrevan a juzgar si no soy "ni de aquí ni de allá". Y es que no puedo negar que el convivir con otra gente me produjo un cambio radical, pero que no se confunda mi gente; ¡Qué la patria duele, sí señor! Y sí, eso ya no vale pa` ser dominicana. Perdóneme usted por discrepar: Lo que une a esta morena a sus raíces es encenderse al primer acorde de un merengue, añorar su comida y su gente, y al poco de encontrarse con otro paisano, allá donde fuese, empezar un parloteo sin igual.

Soy hija o lo fui del sancocho, del pastel en hoja, del chimichurri y el chicharrón, soy o fui hija del plátano frito, la batata asada, del tamarindo y la guayaba.

Siete mudanzas llevo a cuestas y mira que no me pesan, de todas aprendí y son parte de mí. Después de España llegó Alemania donde nace mi primer hijo, y luego Austria donde nace la princesa de la casa. Hoy los educamos en tierra neutral. Buscando para ellos una estabilidad y que tengan el privilegio de echar raíces en algún lugar, y así crear parte de su cultura, entre mezclada inevitablemente con la de sus padres, que ni son de allí ni de allá.

Una vez viviendo en Austria, por pan fui a una esquina de casa, y un hombre corto de miras me observaba. Mientras, yo intentaba que mi hijo mayor no echase la tienda abajo. Después de pocos minutos, me increpó diciendo que por qué hablo a mi hijo en otro idioma que no es el alemán. Yo accedí a responder con educación: Diciéndole que español era mi idioma materno y que era importante para mí que lo aprendiese. Al parecer esa fue la chispa que aquel individuo esperaba para encender su llama y decirme que, gracias a personas como yo, que no enseñábamos a nuestros hijos desde pequeños el idioma nacional, era por lo que las escuelas estaban peor, porque las maestras en vez de tener que enseñar a sumar y restar tenían que enseñar a los niños a hablar. Después de aquello palabras me faltaron para contestar a aquel austriaco, pero me dio más fuerzas para seguir en mi lucha de enseñarle a mis hijos mi idioma, viviera donde viviera. Hoy mi hijo mayor tiene ocho años y habla tres idiomas y va aprendiendo el cuarto.

Soy hija o lo fui de «bendición papi y mami" «¡Concho!" «¡Ven pa' acá!" «¡Qué vaina!" «¡Estoy quilla'!"

Soy un pez de pecera que han tirado a un inmenso mar. Soy un árbol trasplantado que creció en un lugar y ahora es otra tierra la que lo nutre y otro cielo el que lo riega. Soy aquel árbol que no olvida aquella tierra donde germinó, se hizo árbol y hoy agradece al sol que le brilla. Hoy, su mejor abono es aquel lugar que le vio nacer ¡Sí señor!

Cuando vuelvo de visita a la República Dominicana sé que soy distinta. Definitivamente tengo otra manera de ver la vida, pero por ello no me siento menos dominicana. A lo mejor soy una especie algo tuneada para la risa de algún hermano, amiga o primo. De alguna manera tu tierra tiene la fuerza sobrenatural de sellarte y reclamarte suya; tatuarte en el alma que por más que nades, corras o vueles lejos de ella, le sigues perteneciendo. Siento que es algo más allá de lo comprensible, porque al fin y al cabo no fue algo que decidiera, estaba ya escrito.

Más allá de la etiqueta de ser o no ser de un pueblo, un folklore o una nación, esto es algo que decide tu corazón, y va relacionado al amor propio y al de pertenecer a un punto del mapa, sin importar las fronteras, sus mares o sus kilómetros, ni siquiera su belleza, ese punto del mapa te pertenece y tú le perteneces a él.

Soy hija o lo fui de un himno quisqueyano, de tres padres de la patria y una historia de conquistas a la libertad.

Cuando regreso a mi país parece que salgo de una cápsula del tiempo. Antes he dicho que he cambiado, pero la gente que se queda también cambia. El ciclo de la vida sigue su curso y las costumbres van evolucionando. Solo yo me siento atrapada en aquel año en el que partí. El dinero ya no vale lo de antes, palabras coloquiales que yo ya no entiendo, viéndome obligada a preguntar su significado, y es en ese preciso momento en el que me siento como una extranjera estúpida en mi país. Estúpida por ser de allí y no parecerlo. Son realidades que voy aceptando, porque por otro lado también he sabido ganar, sintiéndome según pasan los años que "ni soy de aquí ni de allá"

Soy hija o lo fui de quien dice « voy ahorita» o «dame un chin».

La vida me ha premiado con dos maravillosos hijos y un esposo insuperable, y ahora que soy madre y que he vivido en mis propias carnes el "ni de aquí ni de allá" intentamos educarlos en la cultura de valores. Esos que da igual a donde quieran volar o su rincón encontrar. Serán inequívocos y universales. Raíces fuertes de integridad y de respeto. Así serán bienvenidos a donde vayan.

Mis hijos, mis queridos hijos, que bien se levantan comiendo comida húngara, austriaca, española o dominicana. En Navidad traerán regalos el Divino Niño, Papá Noel o los Reyes Magos. Sin duda habrán cosas buenas y malas de este mejunje de culturas, como todo en la vida, lo importante es cómo lo tomes. Yo he tenido la suerte de amar a un país y su gente, de que me duela y preocupe lo que allí ocurre, y me enorgullezca de sus logros y medallas. Mis retoños tendrán la oportunidad de amar a unos cuantos puntos más en el mapa, solo de ellos depende, ya lo he dicho antes, esto es algo que decide el corazón.

Y si soy hija o lo fui, me respondo a tal cuestión: culturas hay muchas y pocas a las que ames de corazón. Algunos no tienen opción más que amar a una y por omisión. Yo he salido a navegar y mientras más lejos me voy, descubro que soy de un lugar, de una isla bonita, de gente sin igual, y que por más que huya lejos de ella, te aguarda, te espera, y te da un lugar a donde mirar si alguna vez te sientes perdido en este ancho mar. Es por algo que la llaman PATRIA, pues como ella ninguna aguarda paciente, por si algún día decides regresar.

Pero Mañana me Voy - Anabel Soto

Trying to perfect my Spanish,
learning new English words,
fitting in with white coworkers
looking down on *El Diario,*
looking for myself in the *The New York Times.*
my unread issue of *The New Yorker* sits next to Mami's *Vanidades.*
I'm not going to D.R. this summer
I want to go to Miami.
I'm not going to DR next summer
I'm going to Iceland.
When I visit my mother *en El Cibao,*
the locals low key played me
with jokes I didn't understand.
I shrugged,
I'm leaving tomorrow.
I have to return
to my new struggle,
climbing the corporate ladder,
even though the VP's don't look like me.
I have to return to erasing my double negatives
and getting by with fragmented positivity.

In Between Mountains- Quizayra González

I think about Mamá when I trim the leaves on the overgrown plants, or when I burn candles for the souls that need an illuminated path. I picture her sitting at the table, as always, with a phone between her ear and shoulder. She'd pencil in little houses on the edge of her phone book. Each line marked the page with unassuming houses made up of triangles and squares. I often flipped the edges of these pages with my thumb to make the little drawings come alive. Together, the houses created a hypnotic dance that lulled me into recollection.

In between the " no me digas" and the "bueno, eso no se hace," Mamá filled in the edges of her pages with hundreds of unfinished houses. Each of them contained an emptiness that was in stark contrast to the fullness of the hands that created them. An hour or so into her phone call, Mamá pointed to my cell phone with the sly smile of someone that's found a loophole. She would point again so I understood that I was to call our house number, so that she had an excuse to end the conversation.

" Ah sí…¡Me etá entrando otra llamada!" is how she ended all her calls.

As a reward for my part in her mischief, Mamá would ask me if I wanted coffee. I would say yes (for the second or third time that day) and we would sit on the porch, taking in each other's silence. Our coffee rituals didn't have an exact schedule, but they started when we recognized the need for stillness in each other. Some days, Mamá would interrupt the still air and offer me one of her memories.

"I never left el campo before coming here to Philadelphia." She sat with those words for a few minutes with her coffee mug cradled between her small hands.

Mamá said this on a Spring day, while a warm breeze glided through the porch and tousled her signature pleated skirt. I watched her look beyond the small lawns that outlined our block. Her words carried her off to the dusty path that led to her wooden house, on the hill in Corocito, a small village outside of San Jose De Las Matas. As Mamá's shoulders fell and she settled deeper into her chair, she turned to me with a grin and said, "I was born and raised between those mountains." Her eyes glistened with joy—a joy that came from knowing that she belonged to the mountains, and despite the distance, the mountains belonged to her. I try to capture that joy for myself as my tongue curved, coiled and snapped the edges off from each of my words, producing a crisp Cibao accent. Those linguistic flips pull me out of the fringes and tell me that maybe I, too, belong to the mountains; Or that at least I have some kind of inheritance hidden between the peaks. It's been hard for me to claim that heritage for myself sometimes. Her stories give me a momentary reprieve from the margins.

"Mamá, ¿y uté recuerda cómo era Corocito antes?" I asked with a smile and continued. "I remember when I was a child and used to lay on two chairs, while I listened to you pray the rosary in the old house. Do you remember how the porch was blue and made of wood? The chairs were the same blue, with a seat made of cowhide. There was always coffee, even in the middle of the night, for all the people that came to recite the rosary with you. The women stayed near the front and the men towards the sides. The children hung from the porch columns. It was our evening ritual. The rhythmic prayer sounded like chants and spells in my mind."

I let myself get lost in that childhood memory. My mind travels to that blue porch at the end of the dirt road lit by oil lamps. I make a bed out of two chairs and lay on my side to watch the flickering flames. One memory melts into another scene and I'm following my grandmother through a wooded path on our way to the river. With her left hand, she carries a woven basket filled with mondongo. She uses her right hand to clear the branches in front of us. She turns back to me, revealing the sun breaking through the branches and kissing her cheek. Her almond skin glows against the greenery. Her smooth hands and unburdened face tell me that this memory does not belong to me. I am merely a visitor to an open memory that was once offered to me.

I intended to continue my walk but was pulled back by a clank, as my tin mug slipped out of my hand and left a pool of coffee inching towards my feet. I leaned back and placed my bare feet on the porch fence as I listened to my grandmother's giggle. I knew I'd need to make more coffee soon but I sensed Mamá beginning a new story so I settled into my chair.

"¿Tú sabe que mi papá tenía un cafetal? The coffee trees covered about half a mile, all the way to Henaro's land. You know him right?" I didn't but nodded yes so that she would continue. "The cafetal would awaken in April with white flowers, where the scent of roasted coffee danced around us until winter. When I was a young girl I would walk through the cafetal instead of the main road. It was my favorite path to the river but my sisters hated it because there were so many garden snakes. Cobardes"

Mamá chuckled, shifted in her chair, and crossed her right leg over her left, causing her sandal to dangle lightly on her foot. She continued.

"He sold it for 250 pesos. Did you know that? I think that was about four or five dollars. I guess that was a lot of money at that time. One day, he just decided to sell it. He was getting old and he couldn't work the land and my brothers had already moved to the city. He sold it and spent the rest of his days in Santiago. There was no one left to work the land."

"Weren't you there, Mamá?" I asked

"Claro. I told you I never left." She responded.

Her answer ended our conversation and we melted back into silence. I thought about my grandmother's children and their stories. My mother, aunts, and uncles never offer memories of the mountains. They don't talk about cleaning mondongo in the river because we are in Nueva York. Well, we are in Philadelphia, but everything here is Nueva York. They don't want to sound like campesinos so they leave their memories at the airport, some secretly hoping that they will be there when they return. To my mother, the mountains are dusty relics of a wretched life that she keeps buried underneath her American dreams. Despite all this, Mamá says they never went hungry, always had a nice dress for church, and always had enough coffee for visitors. She tells me this country fills us with excess and scarcity. We are in a new land, with more food and fewer rivers, unlimited clothes but nowhere to go, piles of coffee cans but no cafetal. I often think about my place in between these two immovable women, floating between their histories to create a more visible picture of myself.

I got up and sucked my teeth when I stepped on the forgotten pool of coffee. "I guess it's time for another cup, Mamá. This time I'll make it a little lighter and steam some milk. Would you like that?" I didn't wait for a response as I picked up my tin mug and walked past her empty chair. The cool evening breeze ran through the porch and stirred the hanging plants. As I opened the door, the slightest scent of roasted coffee beans entered the house.

Nostalgia - Juana Toribio

Tengo miedo a despertar, abrir los ojos y afrontar mi realidad.
Sonreír me es casi imposible.
Me entristece la distancia;
tu recuerdo me sofoca.
Te llevo incrustada en el alma,
y a pesar de la lejanía, te pienso con todo mi ser.

Te extraño.

Triste partida.
Se me hace difícil admitirlo,
a medida que pasa el tiempo
me arrepiento,
lloro, sufro … muero.

En mis sueños siento tu aura,
el cálido abrazo de tu viento,
veo el fruto de tus jardines,
la esperanza en tu amanecer.

Me equivoqué.

No esperaba esta frialdad,
tanta indiferencia,
el rechazo de mi identidad,
la supresión de mis sueños,
sacrificios, mas ninguno valorado.

Falsas verdades; limitaciones.

Desilusión.

Tras el trayecto
mueren mis sueños y aspiraciones,
familiares, tradiciones,
mi corazón, mis pasiones.

Espero el día en que pueda regresar a ti,

a mi descendencia, al cantar de tus olas,
al familiar rojo de la amapola.

Abro mis ojos, mojados,
testigos de la melancolía
de mi historia gris.

Enjaulada sueño despierta.

¿Y tú hija?- Pamola Valenzuela
(Monologue from "The Pineapple Diaries"
Written for the character of Catalina.
May 2019)

So, I had this serious craving for some bistec con arroz y habichuela the other day. The one from Miami Restaurant. I was right around the corner so I just went in to order take out.
It was raining out that day so I couldn't really kill time walking around the neighborhood- you know, so I just bought a cold presidente and sat at one of the tables by myself.

Raulin was playing so loud on the speakers. There was this group of middle-aged men in windbreakers wearing Red Sox hats huddled together at a table by the window—leaning back in their seats to watch the baseball game that was playing on the screen in the corner behind them.

I looked around the restaurant, noticing the clutter of photographs that use to hang on the walls wasn't there anymore. I realized in that moment that I missed them—that I wished they were still there. But why?

I was awkwardly scrolling through my phone, taking small sips hoping it would last long enough, waiting in a space filled with men. The soundtrack of loud, overly bassed bachata in the background would probably make anyone feel like they had to awkwardly disimular—dique como que ta haciendo algo en su celular.

I kept looking up to la muchachita at the counter. She'd turn around to ask the cook through the metal ventanita if my food was ready. She'd turn back around and shake her head like—"Todavía. ¿Quieres otra cerveza?"

I shook my head "No, gracias." Them rice and beans are worth it though. I just kept waiting. At this point I put my phone down, stopped looking through wedding day to-do lists and took a final sip of my beer. You know that last sip you take just out of habit at this point 'cause there's not really even a drop left.

And I just decided to sit there resting my chin on my hand, looking at the now empty wall.

Just then, a man came into the shop—little pancista, aviator style seeing glasses and one of those 90s style bomber jackets. Not, like, funky, just like, simple in like a muted brown—something you would see Balbuena wear in Nueva Yol.

He seemed surprised to see that group of men near the window. Maybe they use to work together; I didn't quite make that out but anyway, they greet him, "Hey Fulano!" I didn't, I don't remember his name. Anyway, that part doesn't matter. He shook each guy's hand and they did a little small talk. You know, that kind of small talk Dominicans do so well: "Bate, ¿cómo está todo?" "Bieeeeen bieen. Todo tranquilo." "Te mudaste, ¿verdad? ¿Cómo va eso?" "Oh bien, gracias a Dios. Sí. Sí. Sí." "¿Y tu hija?" "Oh bien, bien una maravilla, una maravilla. Ella se mudó también, compró su primera casa por ahi por Salem." "¡Qué bien mi hermano! ¿Y los nietos?" "Oh bieeeen bieeeen, eso muchachito tienen pila de energía. 24/7, 24/7. Sí, sí"

It was comforting to me. I don't know why. It brought a smile to my face just kind of feeling like I knew what this small talk was gonna look like, and it ended up looking just like I had imagined. The dragged out "bien," the repeated "biens," the "gracias a Dios" and "tranquilito."

Fulano kind of patted one of the guys on the back to softly end the conversation.

He hopped over to the counter to pick up his take out order. When he was at the counter, I got a good look at him; his pudgy cheeks, his small crater scars, the grey around his sideburns.

He reminded me of my Dad. Papi lives in DR, taking care of the family business and a couple colmadones. I try to see him every year. We talk as much as we can on the video chat and Whatsapp.

We do that small talk thing all the time.

"Mija, ¿cómo tú ta? ¿Cómo va eso en los Boston?" "Biennn Papi todo bien"

Inthat moment, I had this vision in my head; of my Dad in Santo Domingo, walking into a restaurant to pick up takeout and seeing a group of old friends gathered at a table.

"¡Rodolfo! ¡Oh, Oh! ¡Cuánto tiempo! ¿Cómo va todo? ¿Y la familia? ¿Y tu hija? ¿Y los nietos?"

...and I wondered about what he says. What does he say? Does he tell them real stories? His daughter is divorced, no kids, 31. Does he sugar coat it or just say "bieeen, bieeeen"?

Does he say "she's working hard, just graduated. She's a pharmacist now!" Does he even call it that? Does he say something more general like, "she's in the medical field"? Does he say I'm getting re-married? Does he say any of that stuff at all? Does it stress him out when his friends ask about me or is he proud to talk about me? Does he say he's proud of me? (Beat.)

I don't know. In that moment, I thought to myself, I don't know if my Papi says he's proud of me in those moments of small talk...maybe he doesn't need to say it for me to feel that he is. It just occurred to me how much it would mean to me to know that on any given day, at any moment, when coming across a friend in an unexpected place, that he can say that in some way, I have made him proud.

The Gifts I Brought Back For Her - Paola Cespedes

When I left, I sought awakening
from the sweetness existing
just outside the clouds in my mind.

Now I return to myself,
removing the shattered pieces piercing my bubblegum tongue,
healing my words with the purity of the future I carried
back for her.

Now I return to myself,
surviving a thousand revolutions for you.
My crimson hands are tainted by warfare
between me, myself and I.

Now I return to myself,
nourishing my senses with the nobility of Venus,
offering the planets in my palms to fasten
the stars in my crown.

Now I return to myself,
returning to the rosy lakes of my consciousness,
offering French silky lilacs
to soften the hardened armor of my mind.

Now I return to myself,
offering a kaleidoscope of hues I've neglected to see.

Now I return to myself,
offering a fistful of the forgotten pigments of her soul.
Now I return to myself,
with these gifts I've found for you.

"Written from my mother's perspective as she immigrated to the United States at the age of eighteen years old. These are the gifts she carried back for me."

Entre Luca y Juan Mejía- Ana María González Puente

A la edad de treinta años y con un doctorado en derecho en la espalda y en un momento de semi locura, decidí abandonar la isla, la familia y los amigos y emprender un viaje de ida hacia Nueva York.

La decisión la tomé en gran parte porque estaba hastiada de los apagones y de la doble vida que llevaba vestida con medias de seda y tacos de cinco pulgadas durante el día, mientras que cuando regresaba a casa tenía que bregar con una lámpara o un inversor para alumbrar la noche.

A los pocos meses de estar viviendo en la Gran Manzana empecé a añorar los convites con los amigos, los pasadías y encuentros domingueros en casa de mi madre o de algún vecino, los paseos vespertinos con mis amigas por la calle El Conde para tomarnos un café caliente o una cerveza fría, según el día.

El contraste entre la vida festiva y el encerramiento en un apartamento, aunque acompañada, era palpable. Si no eres fuerte, te destruye.

Sin embargo, quise minimizar el impacto del dramático cambio y me concentré en estudiar en un colegio comunal para romper la barrera idiomática pensando que eso resolvería todos mis problemas. No contaba con el acento que te marca al hablar y te desnuda frente a todo el mundo y te pone una etiqueta que dice «Tú no eres de aquí. Llegaste grande. Se te entiende, pero no eres oriunda», etcétera.

Los días se sucedían lentamente y parecía que nunca iba a graduarme y a terminar y a poder, por fin, trabajar en una oficina, a lo cual aspiraba profundamente. Hasta que un día por fin ocurrió. Pensé que también por fin iba a conocer a los neoyorquinos y que podría entablar amistades e integrarme definitivamente a la cultura americana. ¡Cuán equivocada estaba! En realidad, nadie estaba interesado en hacer amistades nuevas e incorporarme a su mundo. Inclusive, una compañera de trabajo se atrevió a decirme que los nuevos inmigrantes no caben en la agenda de ninguna persona. Es difícil hacer amistades después de cierta edad.

Un tiempo después, estando en el aeropuerto de Burlington, donde había ido a visitar a mi hija a la Universidad de Vermont y mientras conversaba con otra hija, una señora americana que escuchaba la conversación en inglés me preguntó de dónde venía a lo cual contesté que de Nueva York y a lo cual ella replicó —no, de dónde originalmente.

A cada paso, el fuerte acento me delataba. Este día en particular, entendí y acepté que por más que tratara de mejorar la pronunciación y me esforzara por ser aceptada sin reservas, yo no era de aquí.

En lo que respecta al ni de allá, he tenido varios momentos en los cuales me han hecho notar que ya no soy de allá, como cuando regresé por primera vez después de dos años fuera y pegué el grito al abrir la ducha para bañarme al recibir el chorro de agua fría, ante lo cual mi mamá vociferó —Ah, ya te acostumbraste al agua caliente de Nueva York.

En otra ocasión, estando en Punta Cana, una empleada de una de las tiendecitas del resort remarcó —Tú eres dominicana, pero se nota que ya no eres de aquí; hablas diferente.

Asimismo, durante un viaje a Santo Domingo, mi hermana y yo tomamos un taxi para ir al teatro, cuando todo era tinieblas, pues se había ido la luz y yo expresé mi temor al tráfico en medio de tal oscuridad, a lo cual ella contestó —Si tienes miedo de andar de noche sin luz, ya no eres de aquí.

Cada una de estas situaciones, cada uno de estos viajes fue reafirmando el hecho de que realmente empezaba a sentirme que no era ni de aquí, ni de allá. Pero también que tenía que forjar mi propia identidad; una en la cual yo escogiera lo mejor de cada cultura. De aquí, el respeto a las leyes, la justicia, las múltiples oportunidades de superación. De allá, la alegría, la amistad, la hospitalidad. Una identidad *sui géneris,* que en lugar de sentirte como un apátrida emocional que no es ni de aquí, ni de allá, puedas profesar y expresar en altavoz para que lo escuchen en los dos países: —Yo soy de aquí; también soy de allá. Aunque a veces te encuentres entre Luca y Juan Mejía.

Candela - Armando Bautista

That's how my abuelo bit it: Liver gave out. The brown sugar stopped
processing in his processor. Was it Wild Turkey or Old Grand-Dad's he
sipped on? I remember the sweet caramel smell that radiated from him; a
handsome Indio with mustard for the whites of his eyes. He had a
"batmobile" station wagon a la Adam West, but only in cognitive
dissonance; it had red fins and bucket leather seats. We'd ride down
Riverside Drive with his two Doberman Pinschers in the back seat; their
big ol' heads out the windows, tongues swinging. I think Ibrahim Ferrer
was playing on the cassette deck.
"Ay candela, candela, candela, me quemo... Aé..."
That could be my own wishful thinking or conflating the brown sugar
men, who both wore embroidered golf caps. There's that and the Dollar
bill origami shirt he, Wenselao Ramon Batista, made and framed for me.

Later, I used the money to buy a toy of no particular importance. I fucked
up.

The gift of memory still haunts me
Like every time I slide a stack of $1 bills on the bar
After sipping on some brown sugar
"Is this your dollar, abuelo?"
Or, this one?

Mama Created a Ten Year Old Feminist- Yulissa Hidalgo

You would think that growing up with a matriarch head of household meant freedom, choices, and equality—wrong. I remember waking up early on Saturday mornings to the sound of drums, guitars, and Spanish lyrics (singing?) about partying or heartache and *mal de amores.* It was the ultimate indicator that the long list of chores was upon us and our rest was over. Either this or my grandmother barging in to remind us of our weekly duties would wake us up. To be quite frank, I may not be the most organized person in the world, but I find an immeasurable amount of calmness in cleaning to this day.

One day, I got fed up. Why did my autistic sister and I have certain chores while our younger brother had others (don't phrase this as a question. You can just state that y'all had more chores)? It didn't make any sense. My sister and I always did dishes, swept, mopped, and dusted. Our brother only ever had to take out the trash. Where is the justice? Then, the summer before fifth grade started, I had an epiphany.

My confidence was at an all time high because I was being placed in the top class as one of the most improved students in my ESL group. School supplies had already been purchased, and a couple of new uniform shirts too. This was the perfect time to stand up to my grandmother, or so I thought.

I was bold, not foolish. My sister and I discussed our plan to challenge authority during my grandmother's favorite activity—playing cards. After my grandmother let us each win a round and moved on to her usual winning streak, I politely asked, *"Mamá,* why can't I take out the garbage?" She stopped shuffling the cards abruptly and gently placed

98

them on the table. My hands immediately covered my face, but her reaction wasn't physical.

She took a deep breath and said, "*Yo no sé.*"
It was the first time I had ever heard her utter those words. In my eyes, even with a third grade education, my grandmother was an all-knowing being.
She smiled at me and asked, "Why do you want to do it?"
I replied with hesitation, yet spat out words like a panting dog. "I. Just. Want. To. I'm. Stronger. I'm. Older."

She laughed and coughed, then proceeded to light up a cigarette. After inhaling a few times, her reply was filled with bittersweet disdain. "He's the man of the house, *mi negra.*"

For as long as I could remember, she always called me this as a term of endearment and irony. I was the lightest skinned in the family. I took that moment as an opportunity to say the boldest thing I ever told her: "*Mamá,* men don't live here. They leave here." Before I knew it, my palms were covering my mouth.

It was eerily quiet. She put out her cigarette and turned off the music. She dealt the cards and continued to play with my sister and I. It felt like an eternity. She won the round and placed the cards back in the box. She called for my brother who came in cautiously, pretending he was not listening from the kitchen.
"*De ahora en adelante, tú friegas. Yuli, tú sacas la basura. Los hombres y las mujeres pueden hacer lo mismo.*"

In complete shock, the three of us stared at her as she turned the music back on and made her way to the window. She stood there and looked out for a long moment. It was at this precise moment that I learned two valuable life lessons. First, I would always be a feminist, even if it took me eight (more?) years to learn the word. The second lesson was to speak up for yourself, because you never know who you will inspire as a result.

The last in-person conversation I had with my grandmother, I was nineteen years old and back from college for the weekend. It was a cold day in February. Over coffee (hers black with three sugars and mine mostly milk and sugar) we discussed education, sex, and freedom. For someone who was raised in a religious, patriarchal, and traditional household, my grandmother had come a long way. She raised an army of feminists accidentally, but rather meticulously.

¿Qué e' lo que me define? - Mayrenes Figuereo

Mami dice que hablo español como una gringa.
People say I don't look Dominican.
Siento que miento cuando me preguntan:
¿Y tú? ¿Qué eres? (Como si yo fuera un proyecto de ciencia.)
"I'm Dominican."
"Really? I thought you were just black."
"Yeah, same thing."
Same thing, right? Not to everyone.
But I'm not lying. Pero when your people don't believe
in being black,
It sounds like a lie.

"But you're not black like us."
"Pero tú no eres dominicana cómo nosotros."

So, dime, ¿de dónde soy?
¿Qué e' lo que me define?
¿Qué e' lo que me hace dominicana,
  o morena,
  o americana?

My hair doesn't mean anything. My color doesn't mean anything. My
broken-ass Spanish doesn't mean anything.
It doesn't matter because no soy del campo. It doesn't matter because I
didn't grow up listening to Tevin Campbell. It doesn't matter because I
hate yuca. It doesn't matter because I've never had greens. It doesn't
matter because I don't think Boca de Piano is funny. It doesn't matter
because I haven't watched the Friday movies.
It doesn't matter that I'm trying to learn more about the history of my
ancestors. And it doesn't matter that I'm trying to (learn? unlearn? The
sentence is grammatically incorrect as is.) the correlation between the
racism de aquí y allá.

¡Ni me dan crédito por saber, ni me dan crédito por querer saber!
¡No jodan, ya!

¡Ya! ¡Ya!

NI DE AQUÍ, NI DE ALLÁ

Mis padres son de San Juan de la Maguana. I am from Jersey.
De donde vengo y de donde soy are two different conversations.
Al que tenga tiempo, le hablaré.
Al que no me cree:
Espero que la ignorancia nunca tome tiempo para definirle.

Carta a la patria - Gisselle Belia

Algo mío que se queda contigo cada vez que me alejo de ti.

¡Me pierdo! y no busco nada más que el cielo azul entre las alas cuando lejos de ti vuelo.

¡Ah! Suspiro al recordar tu perfume y el olor a agua salada que se quedó en mis labios aún lo puedo percibir.

He pagado un alto costo por distanciarme de ti. Tradúceme los abrazos de mi pueblo que extraño al apartarme de ti.

¡Ay! Yo sola con mis recuerdos y sin poder recuperar nada de lo que perdí, búscame en el archipiélago de donde los veo reír.

El tiempo pasa tan rápido cuando estoy junto a ti que a veces no sé si me voy o te vas de mí.

En la selva me defiendo de mis demonios, ahí en tierra extraña el cielo es gris y pienso en ti. ¡Ahí tu música charlatana se escucha y entre recuerdos me río de ti!

Mangú and Ceviche- Vanessa Pardo

She is the fruit of an immigrant love story; the first generation Dominican-Ecuadorian Latina y la primera hija. Growing up in the concrete jungle, in Little Quisqueya, she always knew she was different. The kids in the neighborhood all seemed to have different shades of brown skin with coils in their hair. She and her brother had thick, black, wavy hair with piercing dark brown eyes and big noses. They were short of stature at 5'1 and 5'5, respectively. Their home smelled of sizzling platanos, red onions, steamed seafood, lemons, and the occasional pancake. Her Mami y Papi swayed, two-stepped and cleaned to Julio Jaramillo, Ana Gabriel, Julio Iglesias, Los Hermanos Rosario, Milly Quezada, Michael Jackson, and the Bee Gees. It wasn't until she entered middle school that she began to understand why she was different.

Her peers made it a point to ask, "What are you?" Instinctively, her face appeared as though she were restraining herself while she processed a million ways to explode. She is still explaining that Ecuador is not a city, state, or anywhere near Mexico, *seriously*. However, while growing up in Washington Heights and later exploring other parts of the United States, she quickly learned it is common to ask this open-ended question when a person appears different from the stereotypes (inappropriate as fuck). In the United States, her answer is Dominican-Ecuadorian. She is not one identity. There is no way she can check one box. She was born into a hyphen.

When she was younger, her Dominican cousins in Washington Heights pointed out she was half Ecuadorian every chance possible; the same went for her Ecuadorian cousins in the Bronx, as though she was never enough for either side. Many degrees and fancy theory textbooks later, she recognizes it as a projection of someone else, but back then, she felt isolated in her experience. Her "identity" had always been dissected without her permission. People were always verbally taking apart her hair, body and mannerisms. One of her favorite comments was when people would say, "I knew you were Dominican, but there was something else." As though she was the main course and they were trying to figure out every ingredient that was used to create her particular look.

It seems to show up as herself never being enough. She needed to explain that her hair really was black and not made by L'Oreal. There was no number on the side of any box with her particular shade, and it naturally grew this long without any oil or home remedies. Her curves weren't from the Dominican side, and, yes, her nose is straight from Ecuador. There was a time she tried to erase one heritage or the other, but it turned out, it was impossible. She was incomplete without one or the other.

The first time she went to the Dominican Republic, she was eight years old. At the time, she did not know much about identity or culture. She simply knew that her Mami was Dominican and Papi was Ecuadorian, because of the homework for culture day at school. She was familiar with Dominican food, music, and the American version of the culture because of her community. The actual country was completely different.

When she arrived in Salcedo, she was automatically labeled "La Americana". In her world, Americans were white, so she struggled to understand her nickname. In the U.S., she used to dance to El General, Selena, and New Kids on the Block. In La República Dominicana, she was required to know Anthony Santos, Johnny Ventura, and Fernandito. Salcedo gave her body permission to move to new rhythms. Her Spanish was forever blessed by El Cibao.

Although she only visited Ecuador once, at the age of two, her father taught them the culture. Her parents raised them to embrace the three cultures. She and her brother are able to hold their own around Dominicans, Ecuadorians, and Americans. Code-switching was real when they were around all three at the same time. To this day, she still pauses, breathes deeply, and recalibrates before speaking.

One of the most important lessons she had to master was the difference between Dominican and Ecuadorian lingo. The most difficult word to keep track of is the Dominican 'ahorita' and Ecuadorian 'ahorita'.

Depending on the parent, she was expected to do something now or later. One time, her father asked her to do something "ahorita," but she didn't respond. "Ustedes no respetan," he yelled as he walked across the apartment. "Hagan las cosas cuando uno les pide" he went on, which confused her because she was going to get to it, just not at the moment. After much yelling back and forth, her Mami finally understood that she was going to do it later, and that she was not ignoring her Papi. He realized that she was confusing meanings. They went on to explain that when he says, "Hagan la tarea ahorita mismo," he means right now. When she says, "Hagan la tarea ahorita," she means later. After many awkward moments, she can finally react accordingly, depending on the parent.

There are also multiple words for different foods, which she learned with family. Her tia called Mami once because she said she loved "guatita" and tía had no idea what she was talking about. "Es suave, se mastica mucho, como rubber," she would say while pretending to chew. Eventually, tía called Mami to understand the Dominican word "mondongo."

Dancing is also a cause for alarm. Her Ecuadorian cousins stare when she dances Dominican music. Although they have pretty good rhythm and dance to all genres, the way she moves her feet and hips during una bachata is just different.

She was born and raised in the land of the free; in la gran manzana. She has bragging rights pretty much anywhere on earth, but it still does not feel like home. At times, the different cultures feel like heavy baggage. In the U.S.A., she is Latina-Americana. In order to earn and keep her "card," she learned about Don Francisco, Walter Mercado, and Cristina. She also had to learn about Sally, Ricki Lake, and Maury. There were times she tried to pretend she did not know one or the other, but it didn't feel right. She attempted to erase parts of herself in order to feel whole or accepted. She thought she could never be enough of one thing, so why try to be all of it. It was clearly impossible.

In her teens, she learned about the Dominican heroines, Las Hermanas Mirabal, and her life was thrown off (changed?) all over again. Learning about Dominican heroines felt natural, as though she was born to be fierce. Her spirit was ignited by the history of her maternal country. She

106

began to read, explore, and step into their footsteps as best she could. Their story taught her about being a guerrera, love, advocacy and believing in herself. Through their story, she was empowered to dig into the story of her family. During puberty, she felt as though she would explode at any moment. Her body and spirit were on fire (partir la boca was sold separately). She did not have the language to express what she was feeling. Her experience always felt as though she was on a rollercoaster. Her brother was the only person she could relate to at the time, but his identity experience was different from hers.

It feels as though her identity is never-ending. Her Dominican abuela loves it when she straightens her long black melena and calls her "La india." If she leaves her hair natural, the Ecuadorians love the way it curls (it's actually curly and wavy, which ain't curly enough for Dominicans). If she speaks Spanish "properly," she is not Dominican enough. If she sounds Cibaeña, she is not Ecuadorian enough. When switching from English to Spanish, she is considered an immigrant.

Visiting La República Dominicana is exhausting because she simply wants to be Vanessa, but somehow, as soon as she walks through the sliding glass doors in the airport, as the humidity smacks her in the face and fucks up her hair, her blue passport marks her for the length of her stay. She visits Queens, NY, Genesis restaurant on 207th street, or parts of NJ to try to find "home" in Ecuadorian restaurants and neighborhoods, but it does not quite fit. Her identity is a never-ending cycle of too much, not enough, and code-switching.

Lucky for her, she has mastered time and place. She can navigate the spaces she is in. She learned to own her identity as a whole, not in parts. She is a gold hoop, red lipstick, high heel wearing woman con una melena and a smart mouth. She comes from a long line of strong, independent, and hard-working women. She loves merengue, salsa, cumbia, reggae, hip-hop, R & B, country music, perico ripiao and bachata. She needs los tres golpes at least once a week. She enjoys ceviche, sancocho, sango and wings. Her pieces are in different lands. Together they make up her heart and soul. Without them, she is incomplete. She will forever be too much or not enough, which is una vaina bien.

Alma Rosa - Gabriela Blanco Bobea

Devuélveme mi casa
aunque sus paredes ya no existan,
que de los escombros recobro el nombre de nuestro río seco.
Devuélveme la tierra donde me halan tus huesos,
donde una luna roja se agazapa entre mis versos,
donde se desangra en blanco un Galán de Noche inmenso,
retorciendo sus raíces bajo un terso cemento…
y la brisa que lo dobla, lo consuela al repetir
que aún sueñan bajo el suelo
las semillas del cajuíl.

Am I a Black Lesbian?- Yoseli Castillo

Here I am again, at a crossroads, in a deep labyrinth, questioning myself. There is a call for submissions for Black lesbian writers and a voice within me telling me to submit. I want to submit, but why should I? How can I claim to be Black if I am a light-skinned Latina?

My lesbianism is not questionable. I love women. I sleep with women. The world I know and the one I write about is permeated by my female body. That aspect of my identity is no longer a conflict nor a crisis, not even when I am in the most conservative or familial spaces in my Dominican or Latino communities. My Blackness though, is problematic, in both the Black and Dominican communities. I know my Blackness does not come from my skin color. My complexion is very light brown. I know it is not from my parents' history with Martin Luther King Jr or the Civil Rights Movement. I am an immigrant.

So, what makes me Black?

It is both my personal experiences and my cultural history, going back to slavery in America, not the United States, the whole continent. In this country, if you are not white, you are Black. This dichotomy makes all people of color fall into the same "other". Categorizing that both includes and erases people like me, a light-skinned Afro-Latina. I also know that white and Black Americans' definition or image of Blackness does not include me; nonetheless, I have been treated less than, expected to achieve less than, and had to prove or fight twice as hard as whites.

NI DE AQUÍ, NI DE ALLÁ

I grew up intellectually, socially and consciously in this country, with fighter-writers such as Audre Lorde, Barbara Smith, bell hooks, Toni Morrison, Gloria Anzaldua and Cherrie Moraga backing me up, teaching me drills and feeding me words. I knew from my early college years that my place was on the margins, that I was an outsider. I could only and truly be myself from that perspective, with my Black sisters by my side. Just like my sexuality woke up in this country, so did my Blackness. It did not happen by virtue of living in the "land of the free," but by my experiences with these writers, the professors who taught me, the classmates who shared ideas, the friends I went clubbing or picketing with, and the colleagues I have argued with throughout the years.

You may say I studied being Black. I believe there are many people with dark skin, Latinos or African Americans, who have not or could not have studied Blackness and are not aware of their ancestors, their fights, and triumphs. I also know many do not need to study it; they wear it and suffer it through the violence inflicted on their Black and brown bodies. I see it every day. I live and work with my Black community, whether it is African American, Afro-Latino, Afro-Caribbean, or African. I live my Blackness every day.

I come from a long line of African queens, midwives and storytellers who were brought to the Dominican Republic over 500 years ago. I know and I live some of their struggles, their stories, their dances, their beliefs, their food. I have some of their hair, their milk, and their hips. Even though my parents or great-grandparents did not fight as hard as Malcolm X and Rosa Parks did, I have my Black fighters too. Here in the United States, we are taught that the first free Black country in the world was Haiti, half of my native island. Since then, and against the overpowering Eurocentric dogma the island has endured, there are and there have been Black fighters on both sides of the island. Sebastián Lemba, Mamá Tingó, Papá Liborio, José Francisco Peña Gómez, and Sonia Pierre are some that come to mind right now in the Dominican Republic.

A person should not identify with anything in a vacuum (and one's brain can be a vacuum). Even though identity is individual and personal, it is relative to environment and experience. If we are somewhat mentally healthy social beings, one's idea of self needs to be made relevant to others, whether it is accepted or rejected. I could say I am a bird, attempt to live as one, and demand recognition as such, but my mental health will be questioned. Also, in our society, there is no space for a "human bird" to functionally live and thrive. Now, racial identity is different. We have built and structured our modern societies based on race, to benefit one group over another. Because race is a social construct and identity is personal, the margin for error (or I would say for creativity) is enormous. We have seen white people pass as Black (???) and vice versa. We have Rachel Dolezal and the white-dark-skin Dominicans (these are not good enough examples to make this assertion). What makes either one real is the experience, both for the individual and for the community that individual lives in. Dolezal lived as a Black woman for many years in her circles. White-dark-skin (what does this mean?) Dominicans have a place in the Dominican Republic and in their Dominican communities in the diaspora. For those of us who are aware of how the concept of race was created and continues to be used to keep a group in power and others powerless, we know how deeply disturbing these racial identities are. Therefore, calling myself Black or Latina or lesbian or a woman, I believe is valid. I have assumed these identities. I have experienced them. They have been validated by my communities.

I do know some people may not accept my label and question it or reject it. It has happened many times and in different social circles. Once, a respected Black scholar and acquaintance called me white. It was a heated discussion in which she implied I was stealing an identity, taking advantage of it, and I had no right to claim Blackness. Due to studies and reflections on my Blackness, I learned of the rights, privileges, and responsibilities I hold in this country and to whom I owe them. I know some of the names and the stories of those who sacrificed their lives for the future they dreamed, that I am living today. That's why the life I live, the job I do, the poems I write are a part of that legacy; they are committed to a better future for all Black lives, including mine.

I know the reputation Dominicans and most Latinos have of denying our Blackness, but there is a long history of Black pride, primarily practiced through the religion, music, and food of the descendants of enslaved Africans brought to the island. This Black pride is not by any means mainstreamed, nor has it created a civil rights movement like in the United States, yet there are many women and men who have fought and died for the rights of Black Dominicans in the Dominican Republic.

So, I am a proud Afro-Dominican lesbian. I am going to submit.

*This piece was also published in the Sinister Wisdom 107: Black Lesbians -We Are the Revolution!

My Roots - Rosina Roa

I stay up late listening to a an enchanting melody,
its words and imagery ravish my mind
the mirage blows a gentle wind.
I lay comfortably on my hammock,
swinging to and fro.
My Caribbean benevolence
courses through my veins,
changing blood into favorable spices.
El valor de comprender el
motivo de irme para mi terra bella,
continúa siendo la mejor conclusión
a mi vida terrenal.
El pueblo con su alma
enorme e illuminada.
La tierra del sazón,
de mi piel y corazón.
Dominicana como las palmeras,
that will always be me,
desde las hojas hasta la raíz.

Assimilation Annihilation - Yadira Ileana Grullón

Assimilation reeks
of fractured spanglish
over bachata beats.
A foreign tongue
barred from public speaking.

Curly bleached hair
burned to a sleek.
Parenthetical smile
for coal whitened teeth.

Taino skin shed
with the seasons.
Repercussions
part of the reasons.

A lost soul whitened with conceit,
or a survivor disguised to conquer feats?
A prisoner of opportunity
must not be confused for a minority.

Assimilation reeks
of caged children
their futures bleak,
indoctrinated in a failed
democracy.

Insidious racist policies,
see us fit in
rather than disagree.

"I was born here, they won't come for me."
Assimilation complete.
The diminution of me.
Annihilation
of the Latinx,
Dominican, we.

To Mami, Harry Potter, and Aventura- Greisy M. Genao

Somewhere in my memory my mother sings "Cuándo volverás" by
Aventura to a boiling pot of rice. She could be begging for the return of
four people.

I am 10 years old and reading Harry Potter again. My mother
pica cebolla en la cocina. My eyes itch. Cedric Diggory dies and I am
crying. Mami knows but doesn't come to check on me. She knows I
don't like being acknowledged.
El amor de madre es algo fuerte como Café Bustelo a las 9:15 de
la mañana.

When I was
little, admito que tuve una obsesión con hablar el inglés mejor que
el español, although neither mattered because all the spells are in Latin.
Con mi hermanita fue lo contrario. Ella y yo somos like day and night.
She never forgets how to say the word "cup" in Spanish. In my memories
I'm not Dominican enough, but my sister is.

I read that Harry's parents were murdered while he sat in
his cuna. Yo era un chichi de tres meses the first time I visited
la República Dominicana—for the burial of my grandparents.
My abuelo died because his heart was too big for his chest. In the spirit
of irony, I become a poet. Dile al amor that my grandmother died two
days after him because of heartbreak. In the spirit of irony, I remain a
poet.

NI DE AQUÍ, NI DE ALLÁ

I returned to Quisqueya when I was 22. I don't read for fun anymore and my mother hasn't been back since her little brother died. She doesn't know the river near her home in Baitoa is drying out. I don't tell her.

When I look at her, pienso, yo quisiera amarla como all the things that couldn't. A love larger than my father, el perdedor que mide 6'1. In the books I find no potions to make him stay. With a wooden spoon in her hand, mami stands at the door and says, "Tú lees demasiado, por eso tienes el español tan machucao." Mami doesn't want me reading esa brujería. She tells me if I keep reading in the dim light, the books will ruin my vision and I wonder if she looked into the future.

In the seventh and final book, Harry acquires a stone that lets him speak to his dead parents and I what is the connection between these two ideas? used to hear mami pray in the dead of night, rezándole a un angelito que le ayude con sus lágrimas. She cries over the cebolla in the pot and the tears work like oil. I close the book and think, Hogwarts could never smell like this. Por un segundo, everything is heaven and onion.

Atlántida - Gabriela Blanco Bobea

Era mi tierra
un rompecabezas
de cinco corazones inundados.
Cinco cacicazgos
redundando en carcajadas
de cataratas insaciables;
donde hoy balbucean ríos
como peces ahogándose de sed.
¿Quién fue que nos cantó el cuento
de las orillas alegres e inalcanzables?
Recuerdo que hablaba con la voz de
las cosas pequeñas e imperceptibles,
reino submarino floreciendo bajo una tierra preñada de sal y de miel.
Hechizo entretejido
por caudales sanguíneos
de pactos milenarios,
desembocando encarnaciones
de guerreros arrodillados
y de ciguapas encadenadas
como mascarón de proa
a la nave temporal.

Like An Old Tree- Danny Jimenez

The sun rose and the sky seemed to be set ablaze. The scorching light crept through the bedroom window and reanimated us one by one. I was hit by the light first, so I rose from my Teenage Mutant Ninja Turtle bed like Dracula rising from his coffin. Then, I looked over to my left as the light swept across my middle brother, who was snoring in his X-Men themed bed. The light finally crept across my youngest brother, sprawled out with a twitchy foot hanging out from under the covers on his solar system themed bed. This day wasn't like your typical middle school day. I was now a senior, Top Dog, and the second person from the immediate family to have the opportunity to go to high school.

My house was different from your typical American household. It was dominicano hasta la tambora! There was a big Dominican Flag hanging in our bedroom, and Mami had an altar in her room that was dedicated to Jesus, which had velones for the different saints. Papi owned a guitar, a güira, and even a piano accordion. *Sometimes I wondered if he was a secret member of a Dominican Mariachi band.* I shook the thought out of my head. I ran out of the room, but hesitated and ducked back in to make sure that my brothers were fully coming from their slumber. The last thing I needed was Mami on my back.

I developed an affinity for Dr. Seuss over the past year, and referred to my brothers as Thing 1 and Thing 2. Thing 1 was my middle brother. He was known for being athletic and having an abyss for a stomach. He'd binge on food the way people nowadays binge on Netflix, and get this, he didn't gain a pound! I was jealous of his supernatural ability. I, on the other hand, gained weight if I stared at a cheeseburger too long. Thing 2 was the youngest of us, known for his ability to befriend people, animals, and probably trees in seconds. We joked that he'd be the

118

Hispanic Steve Irwin when he grew up. He had medium-length black hair and baby blue eyes, which he adorned with black-framed 3D movie glasses that had the lenses popped out. Thing 2 believed the glasses would give him a more sophisticated appearance, and honestly, he was a lab coat short of looking like a little scientist. He spent most of his time watching the discovery and science channels, which was kind of odd for a 10-year-old, but it made him wiser than his peers. Thing 1 and I shuffled to queue up to use the bathroom after Mami and Papi.

"Why are you smiling?" asked Thing 1, as his head tilted in the same way a puppy does when they are confused.

"You mean Mami didn't tell you?" My smile widened. "Well, today is my big audition for a specialized high school. I've been working on my portfolio for the past two weeks." My chest puffed out with pride.

"Oh, I thought you sat around and drew the house plants because you were bored" said Thing 1, exploding into laughter. My face flushed a crimson red.

"What school are you auditioning for?"

"LaGuardia. It's also known as the Fame school. It's where a lot of famous actors, dancers, musicians, and artists have gone."

"Cool, so why are you going..." he says, barely able to contain himself. Thing 1 was then shoved aside by a blur. "Hey! What the—"

"I drank too much water!!!!" said Thing 2, as he whizzed by.

While my brothers and I spoke to each other in English, we would speak to our parents in Spanish or Spanglish. Even though I grew up in a Spanish speaking household, English just came naturally to me due to the consistent practice I had since starting school. Mami would take every opportunity to correct my Spanish, adding the line, "Si no sabes decirlo en Español, dilo en inglés." The funny thing is that I did that to her with English, and we mutually benefited from correcting each other. That didn't stop frustration from creeping in often, when I would speak to Mami and she would start grinning if I had trouble translating something from English to Spanish. I felt like she conditioned me, because whenever she would flash that grin, I would hear her voice in my head saying, "Pues dilo en inglés." My Spanish is still not as good as my parents', which makes me feel a little out of place at home.

--

I ended up being the last one to use the bathroom. As I walked in, it seemed like a hairy creature had made his nest there. There was short, stubby hair in the sink and long strands circling the bathtub drain. Maybe my parents were werewolves. Maybe my parents were going to surprise me with my very own Chewbacca for my birthday. I was hoping for the latter. Not even two minutes into my bathroom routine, I heard a thunderous, god-like voice in the other room.

"¡Daniel Cecilio Jiménez, ven para acá ahora mismo!" Hearing your full name called out was akin to a bad omen. What Gods could I have possibly upset this time? I never fully understood why she named me Danny. She never calls me by that name.

"¿Qué pasó, mami?" I said, waltzing into the living room, trying to make myself appear small.

"Vas a llegar tarde a la escuela si sigues caminando con la cabeza en el aire. ¡Ponte la ropa y sal!" She flashed me that look, you know the one. The "test me boy, I dare you, I'll feed you to your Papi" look. I did not want to be on the menu. You see, in my house, Papi was king of the castle and ruled with an iron fist. Papi moved around like a politician. He was the judge and Mami was the jury. This system was rigged against us from the beginning, so my brothers and I knew to fall in line, lest we upset the jury and in turn, the judge.

"I won't be late porque Pokémon is still on. I'd risk being late if Saved by the Bell was..." I scurried to my room to hear the theme song of Saved by the Bell blaring from my TV, "...on." I rushed around the room like the Tasmanian devil, grabbing socks, a shirt, and my shoes.

"¡Se te olvidaron los pantalones!" Mami bellowed. Would you believe me if I told you she was the calm one of the two?

"¡¿Me tengo que poner pantalones?!" I snickered. She shot me the death stare. Mami was definitely half Jedi. Her stares were on point and worked every time. I proceeded to jump around in my Superman underwear hopping on alternate legs trying to maintain balance as I slid my pants on. I fell twice before I was successful.

--

As the 1 train pulled up on the 66th St station, I tried to store as much visual information as possible; telling Thing 1 and Thing 2 about my experience was going to be the second highlight of my day. Those metal snakes were transporting people through tunnels the way blood travels through veins. It was like The Magic School Bus without the bus, or Ms. Frizzle. As I walked up the stairs to the street level, the new world unfolded in front of me. There was an annoyingly loud humming noise, as if someone had wound up a hornet's nest. To my surprise, it was just a crowd of people, all talking at the same time, incoherently. The blocks down here were longer than what I was used to; it was a lot to take in. I proceeded towards the school building, and was astonished by the monstrous crystal-clear windows that let you peer into the vast lobby of the school. There was a statue, works of art, and banners hanging in the lobby. All of the kids auditioning were queuing up by the entrance, as if we were about to gain entry to some exclusive club on the St. Marks strip. This was the first time I had ventured outside of my immediate neighborhood, so seeing a lot of Asian kids was surprising. The biggest congregation of Asian people I've seen up to that point in my life was inside of a Chinese Food store. There just wasn't that many Asians in Dyckman. As I was running through possible audition questions in my head, I felt a tap on my shoulder.

"Did you go anywhere for summer vacation?" Then, the tall, auburn-haired girl wearing a yellow sundress said, "My name's Sophie."

"Uhh, Hi," I answered with a raised brow. "For summer vaca…"

"I just came back from Milan with Father." She blurted out before I could answer. *This girl talks funny.*

"I went to the park and had some water balloon fights with my friends," I said as a frown crept across her face. She wasn't amused by me at all. I thought that was a pretty good way to spend the summer. She turned around and started talking to a freckled-faced, blond-haired girl behind her. She was a lemming in comparison to Sophie and seemed much more responsive by showering her with oohs and aahs.

NI DE AQUÍ, NI DE ALLÁ

The thing is that back then, I didn't really consider going to the Dominican Republic for vacation. That is why I never really brought it up in conversation. My experience visiting DR every summer always felt strange. I would stay with Papi's family, and because he was well known by his family and campo, I would be made to feel like a celebrity from the time I got there, until the time I left. I'd get showered with attention: "Oh, tú eres Danny, hijo de…," followed by a combination of food, money, and hugs. After seeing past my stature in proximity to Papi, the same people would label me as a "Yankee" for knowing English and being from Nueva York, Nueva Yol as they like to pronounce it.

I was also into different things that the stereotypical Dominican wasn't really into back then, at least not upfront. I was into epic fantasies, writing, video games, and art, while most of my cousins were into drinking, karate, Dominoes (Bones in the states), riding pasolas and motores, and chasing girls. It was weird to be around them because on one hand, they'd want me to teach them English words to impress girls with, but on the other, they'd side-eye me as if to say "él cree que es mejor que nosotros…" Whether it was being in the US and being only able to speak to my parents in Spanish, or being in DR, where I was simultaneously praised for being related to my father and looked down upon for knowing English, I just never felt like I completely belonged anywhere. I was too Dominican for the Americans and too American for the Dominicans. Ni de aquí, ni de allá.

The waiting in line was pretty quiet from there on out. I stood there reflecting on what had driven me to the audition. I had been doodling as far back as I can remember. Papi would work late shifts and slept in the afternoon so Mami could take me with her to BMCC. I'd sit in the back, doodling until her class was over. Even her professors were impressed with my ability to mimic what I was drawing. In 5th grade, I entered a drawing contest, but ended up in second place. One of the art teachers in the school, Mr. O'Shaughennessy, was one of the judges and was impressed by my work. Up to that point, I had been a self-taught artist. He pushed for me to be added to his art class because he wanted to refine the potential that he had seen. I never entered a drawing contest after that. My art did get better, but I loved the competition between my peers and I more than the constraint of an art contest. What kept me improving at a steady pace was my friends, who eagerly awaited a new piece from me. I knew I had arrived as an artist when I started being commissioned to draw cartoon/anime characters by them.

My reflection was disrupted by the sudden movement of the line. It was like the doors to a store hosting a Black Friday sale had opened. They marched us around like farm animals until we reached the first part of the audition. We handed in our portfolios and sat in the cafeteria for our first drawing prompt. The prompt was vague but simple. Draw a logo and label for a soda bottle, be as creative as you want, but don't reference existing material. I didn't know the process behind auditioning, so naturally, I thought the day was over after the first prompt but there was more to this Animal Farm. We were all herded upstairs, bit by bit, into a room that had a tablecloth with some items thrown about, haphazardly on top.

"Grab any seat you'd like and await instruction," said the judge of my future. I sat down and fixed my shirt, which had rolled up due to the weirdly shaped seats. The chairs looked like the letter "L" laid on its side and the short end of the letter was supposed to be the part supporting your back. I changed my seat twice.

"You will be drawing the objects in the middle of the room from your perspective. Please include the table and the tablecloth or you're automatically disqualified." The judge puffed out his chest, as a hyena-like smirk slid across his face. He seemed amused by our bewildered expressions. Then, he started pacing around the room. As he kept passing me by, beads of sweat trickled down my forehead, making a swan dive onto my lap. After the intense showdown with Warden Judge Dredd (lol), we were given a break and told to hang around in the hallway for the final portion of the audition: The portfolio review. The hallway was incredibly spacious. The walls were adorned with still life drawings of various hues and the corners of the hall had student-painted pieces on them. I overheard some of the other auditioners talking out loud, saying things like, "I wonder if they worked in complete silence? Did they have natural light or was it fluorescent? Did they use acrylic paint or pastels?" Being the inexperienced artist that I was, I went up close to the wall to see if I could tell what they were talking about. I started touching them, which didn't help at all. The room went silent and when I turned around, I noticed that I had drawn wild stares from the other candidates. *How was I supposed to know that you weren't supposed to touch a finished painted piece?* The other kids started rambling, so I decided to listen in:

"I've done mock interviews with my Mami, I'm not nervous," I overheard a short chubby kid with rosy cheeks and a flannel shirt tell another. *I was supposed to prepare for this? Like other than working on my portfolio? Crap.* I waited for their conversation to be over and then proceeded to walk towards him.

"I overheard you say that you practiced with your Mami, how'd you do that? My Mami doesn't really know English, so that's not something I could have done."

"My Mami doesn't know much English either, so lo hicimos en Español," said the kid with a grin, as he dabbed beads of sweat off his brow.

"Damn, I should have done lo mismo, my name's Danny by the way…" I said as I wiped my clammy hands on the back of my shirt and out of his field of view, before extending it out to him.

"Me llamo Alex, nice to meet you Danny. You know, I've noticed that no hay muchos muchachos como nosotros…" he said as he peered over my shoulder.

"Yeah and the kids que estan aqui are very different. One told me that she went to Milano and I was so confused. No entendí her excitement over visiting una galleta…" I said holding my forehead and shaking my head. Alex and I both burst into laughter. A minute later, he was called in by Mr. Dredd for his audition. I hoped to see Alex around; he was a cool guy.

"Hey man, are you nervous?" asked a squeaky voice that I couldn't see.

"Umm, no…" I answered checking the corners of my eyes while utterly confused as to whom or what I was answering to.

"You're sweating," said the phantom as he revealed himself, stepping out of what seemed like a dark abyss. The kid was short, had a mushroom bowl haircut, and was sporting horn-rimmed glasses. "You're not very convincing…"

I windshield wiped the sweat off of my brow, as Mr. Dredd popped his head back out into the hallway, locked eyes with me and beckoned me to the dungeon—I mean classroom.

"Come in, sit down. Your portfolio review will start in a couple of seconds." Phew! Good. He isn't my portfolio reviewer. As I sat there, distracted by the splatters of paint in the sinks and the huge blank canvases on wooden canvas racks, a lady manifested in the corner of the room. *Was she there the whole time? Am I in Hogwarts?!*

"I have reviewed your portfolio," she paused. "There are a couple of great pieces here but there's one in particular that I'd like to ask you about." *Oh, this doesn't look good. I was a bear caught with his hand in the beehive. Must have been my self-portrait, I knew using almonds to make the eyes was a short cut but I didn't think someone could pick up on it by just looking at it! Or maybe it was the tree that I drew. Granted I based it off a piece of broccoli, but what's the difference, really!*

The reviewer pushed her falling glasses back to the bridge of her nose and continued, pointing to the golden dragon that I drew. "This piece here… what inspired you to draw this? What emotions were you feeling while working on this piece? Was there music playing while you were working on this?"

"This piece? The Golden Shenron?" I asked with a confused look that only a Mr. Potato Head doll could have given.
"What? I'm talking about this dragon piece; it looks similar to a traditional dragon drawing." She folded her hands in anticipation for the answer I might give. *Emotions? Inspiration? Was there music playing? What the hell did any of that have to do with me drawing this cool looking dragon?* Now the floodgates were open, and I started to produce enough sweat to rival Niagara Falls.

"I didn't feel any emotions. I wasn't playing music and nothing in particular inspired me to draw this dragon other than showing it off to friends, since it was cool looking." I shifted in my chair and dried my hands on my shirt.

"That's interesting, *very* interesting." She scribbled down notes while she continued to mumble to herself. So, this must be what it must feel like to talk to a psychiatrist. Not an experience I'd like to have again anytime soon.

--

That was the end of the auditioning process. I went home not feeling ecstatic, but not completely devoid of hope either. Just being able to audition was akin to getting a golden ticket to Willy Wonka's Chocolate Factory. I felt so out of place as a Dominican kid in an artistic space. I did, however, enjoy meeting Alex and hoped that I'd meet him again, or at least more kids like him. In the words of my favorite hero, Han Solo, "It may not look like much, but you got it where it counts, kid." I bumped into Thing 1 as he was getting home from basketball practice. I filled him in on my trip to Hogwarts and all the colorful characters I met.

"They asked me some weird questions about my Golden Shenron picture. It felt awkward and weird."

"What was weird about it?" Thing 1 asked, giving me a side glance.

"Well, they asked what emotions, music and inspiration led me to making that picture."

"Man, they just wanted to crack your head open and count the rings," said Thing 2 as he shot me a stern look.

"What...?" We turned in surprise. Thing 2 had been listening in on our conversation.

"They wanted to see if, as an artist, you were beyond your physical age. You know, like an old tree. I'm 10 and even I could see that." Thing 2 shook his head and walked away.

"Damn, I think he would have done a better job than you at the portfolio review," said Thing 1 as he burst into tears from laughing so hard.

--

Aquí, especias con sabor a nostalgia - Bremda Acosta

Hace diez años
Que no has visto una jagua
Piensas en decirle a tus colegas que
La jagua se deja trasnochar en el agua
Pero
Cómo se dice trasnochar en inglés
Lo busco en Google y después vuelvo al *breakroom*
Mami dejaba la berenjena quemarse en una hornilla
Luego la descascaraba y la guisaba
Berenjena guisada con arroz blanco y habichuela roja
A dónde diablos se consigue eso en Bushwick
La quemarán en una hornilla aquí también
La hará un chef dominicano con especias olor a nostalgia
Y a veces te preguntas
Por qué nadie te advirtió
Que Lomas de Cayenas te descompondría al más no poder
Pero cómo traduces cayenas al inglés
Cómo se vive aquí sin el allá

The Dominican Runaway- María Ligia Rivas

I was born and raised on the island. My parents are Dominican. My grandparents were Dominican. My great grandparents were also Dominican. No grandfather from Germany or
Italy. No *abuela castiza* from Spain[1] to brag about to my friends. No absent parent living and working in the States. I am, what you would call, *una dominicana de pura cepa.*

A typical poor, middle-class Dominican.

The middle class is a beast of its own, in a mostly poor country, with insanely rich families. The dichotomy between being poor or rich is simple: when you're poor, you're poor; when you're *podrío en cuarto,*[2] you're rich; That's it, as simple as that.

Class on that godforsaken island is so complex that even saying the middle-class has three main levels or categories is an oversimplification, which I feel obliged to use for the sake of brevity:

First, you've got the rich middle class. These people think they're rich and would do anything to prove it, but deep down they know they aren't. Imagine your high-school crush, José Armando; *Rubio,* although not necessarily blond; *cabellito bueno* slickly combed backwards, with skin lighter than most, crisply tanned like a fresh cinnamon roll out of the oven. You would always see him wearing his lucky black Callaway cap, the one that helped him win his last golf tournament, a fitted polo shirt, pressed jeans, a shiny pair of moccasins and a self-sufficient smile completed his everyday look; A natural leader. He was the first in the pack to get a brand new car at sixteen and to go to Paris to improve his nonexistent French, even if it meant taking another mortgage out on that beautiful house in Los Cerros. H was the incarnation of the perfect *chambelán* for the *Quinceañera* party you never had or never were invited to.

Then, you've got the middle-middle class; The back and bone of the Dominican economy. Hard-working people for the most, blessed with a sheer of good luck for the rest (this needs to be retranslated so it makes sense). Remember that girl you met at la PUCMM[3] during your freshman year, who smelled of vanilla and vervain? Carolina. She was always friendly to you and seemed to have lots of acquaintances. She was the perfect size, petite. She once mentioned that she used to be a ballerina when she was younger. Her long, dyed hair is always blow-dried straight, and her bright cherry nails are properly done—the fruit of her weekly pilgrimage to the *salón*. You've never seen her sweat or say something out of place. Although she doesn't have a car yet, her dad, a lawyer or a doctor, fills in as the *de facto* chauffeur, taking her everywhere.

Then, there is the poor middle class. They are not exactly poor by third-world standards, nor are they exactly middle-class by first-world standards. Imagine yourself or me, for that matter. *Morenita*, taller than your average *dominicana*, with frizzed *azabache* hair (damn you, humidity!), surviving on passed down clothes but always looking fresh, even if we had to bathe *con un jarrito porque se fue el agua*. A fan of Kundera and Philip Roth blasting that post-punk revival band I love over the *bachatón* coming from the loudspeakers inside the sweat-smelly *concho*[4] I usually take to get somewhere. I have never set foot inside Disney World and love to use words bigger than my parents' bank accounts.

Being poor middle class on the island is fucking boring. Apart from the occasional summer camps my family could afford when I was growing up, nothing of excitement happened during my summers. The only exception was when my cousins or *tíos de los países*[5] would come to visit.

When they had to leave, I wished I could leave, too. Even so, I knew it was not that simple. When I was a kid, this realization would translate into me crying with *jipíos* at the Puerto Plata airport; and on the way back home to Santiago, not understanding why I could not go with them. Growing up, the crying was replaced by a feeling of being trapped on an island that I always thought I did not belong to.

This feeling gave me purpose. Right after my first American visa application got rejected (I was nine), I had a specific goal in mind: to get off the island as soon as I could before the boredom of my middle-class existence caught up to me and swallowed me whole.

So, I made a plan to get out. I would finish school and then complete a degree at the only university any respectable middle-class *santiaguero* would go to. Then, I would try to get a scholarship to complete a masters degree anywhere but there, manage to find a job or fall in love, whichever came first, and never look back.

That's how with no money, a bit of brains and a lot of determination, I settled for Law School. I tried to find a scholarship to go to a) the US or the UK, b) France, or, c) Spain. Things, of course, weren't easy. Option A did not work out, although it came close. I did not let this small setback stop me. Once I knew option A was a dead end, I put everything in motion for option B.

To this day, I still cannot believe my luck. Everything happened so fast. From the moment I received the rejection letter from the British Embassy in the Dominican Republic, stating that though my application was great, they had given the only two available spots to two brilliant, rich middle-class applicants, to finding myself boarding an Air France flight with a one-way ticket. It happened fast—*más rápido que lo que dicen berejena,*[6] to be precise.

My last day on the island was a Thursday in early September. The aroma of the coffee *recién colao* in the kitchen lingered in the air, while mosquitoes waited around like kamikazes ready to attack. It was a normal day, except that it wasn't. My heart was light and my hands were busy packing the rest of my oversized bag, while Charles Trenet's "*Y' a de la joie*" played on a loop in the background. France was in the air *and* in my immediate future.

As I was walking out of the house, where I spent most of my teenage years, I surprised myself by crying. This was ironic considering the fact that I hated that house with all of my being. My mom dragged me and my two brothers there because she couldn't afford to live anywhere else after separating from my father. It was an old, one-story house in a part of town nobody liked to visit. With its low fence, aluminum windows, and the most hideous floor tiles you've ever seen in your life, this house, also known as *la casa de abuelita*, felt like the place all dreams came to die. Not even *la mata de guayaba* in the backyard could save it.

I know that house was not impressed by my exploit. I was no pioneer. It had already witnessed the departure of two of my mother's siblings, tía Belkys and tío Robert years ago, when they left to try and find a better life in New York. Now it was my turn. The tears slipped down my face and crept into my mouth. I knew the salty taste must be the taste of triumph. I would never see that ugly house again.

A couple of years following my departure, the owner of the house asked my *abuela* to leave after more than thirty years of dutifully paying rent. My family moved a couple of houses further up on the same street. My *abuela* would not leave the neighborhood. The house was demolished, and with it, *la famosa mata de guayaba*. In its place stands a three-story Frankenstein of a building, with a tall fence around it. So yes, I cried because this was a defining decision. I cried because I was finally free.

My little brother, Nuni, who was eleven at the time, cried too when he, my mom and my *tía* Arelis left me at the airport that day. My mom managed to get her boss/rich *tío* to lend her a *jeepeta*[7] with a *chofer,* so we could make the trip from Santiago to Las Américas. Nuni kept banging his head against the passenger seat while we cruised the dusty and battered Autopista Duarte; after which we were swallowed by the sea of cars in *la capital.*

Nuni and I were thick as thieves. Although I am twelve years his senior, it was love at first sight when I saw his chubby face. When he was a baby, I would sit him up on a bed and use him as an audience while I recited the properties of the elements in the periodic table. He trusted me so much that he once let me cut his hair, even though it ended in disaster and my mom had to take him to a barbershop to get a good-old buzz cut. As soon as he was able to read subtitles, we binge-watched the whole reboot of the Doctor Who series on my purple laptop.

NI DE AQUÍ, NI DE ALLÁ

While we breathed the recycled air inside the *jeepeta,* we eyed each other and in that moment, we both knew. I was leaving him behind to succumb to poor middle-class boredom. I could see the spark in his brown eyes fading. The truth is, he wouldn't speak to me over the phone for the next three years.

I understood him. He was right, I left him behind; but this was something I needed to do to prove to him that if I could, he could do it as well. I needed to prove to myself that it was possible to leave the island behind and decide for the first time in my life where I wanted to be.

When I got to France, new adventures awaited me. Besides the usual challenges of academic life in a foreign country, other challenges came as well. For example,, I was not expecting my dominicanness, or my lack thereof, to be a challenge. Unlike its neighbours (Spain, Italy or Switzerland), France, or specifically the South of France, has a relatively miniscule Dominican diaspora. That means the French don't have a particular stereotype about Dominicans. Statistically speaking, we are insignificant.
There are probably two things the average French person might have heard about the Dominican Republic: Punta Cana, which to most was considered a separate country, and bachata, for the lovers of exotic dances like salsa and kizomba. The French stereotype that I felt I couldn't live up to was that of the easy-going, fun-loving, sexy latina, a stereotype any other *dominicana* would have excitingly embraced (this is an odd assumption and a sweeping statement, try to avoid those in your writing.

Dominicans are known to be loud, *todólogos,*[8] party people, great dancers, talkative, superb cooks, so on and so forth. The truth is I am the epitome of undominicanness. For starters, I am a terrible dancer. I was born with two left feet. I don't know how to dance merengue, *mucho menos bachata.* When people asked me how on Earth I didn't know how to dance if I came from the Dominican Republic, I would jokingly say that that was the secret reason my parents sent me off to Europe: They were ashamed of having a daughter that didn't know how to dance; A daughter *que de seguro se iba a quedar jamona.*[9] So they diffused the shame by sending their spinster daughter far away, to Europe.

I am also quiet and reserved most of the time. I only speak my mind when I feel I absolutely have to. If I feel I don't, then I can be silent for

132

hours, just listening. Most importantly, I didn't miss the island one bit, and yet every day, I was confronted with a question that I cannot seem to get answered. *Where are you from?*

The question was simple and some people were naturally curious. *Where was I from?* Does it really matter? Am I from one of the French islands overseas? Why, because I was fluent in French, but had an accent and brown skin? North Africa: Tunisia, or Morocco, maybe? Lots of grandmas have approached me at the bus stop to speak to me in Arabic, mistaking me for one of their own. Central Africa, or Miami when they heard me speak in English. Cuba or Brazil were my personal favorite guesses.

I have had to correct people or explain to them that I came from the Dominican Republic every single time. Although I was reluctant to go into too much detail, there was a part of me that wanted people to get it right. I felt obliged to explain to them that not everyone back on the island was an impostor, like me. People were usually louder and easy going. I gave these explanations as if I wasn't Dominican enough, as if Dominicans couldn't be nerdy, quiet or shy. These interactions revealed that I never felt like a true Dominican, yet I had a passport and a visa status that reminded me almost every day of where I was from.

What makes *me* Dominican? Is it the fact that I was born and raised there? Is it the way I speak Spanish? The cultural references? The common history? The sense of community I should get from being around my fellow Dominicans? Is it that I know what *papaupa de la matica* means?[10] What makes me more Dominican than a foreigner that has fallen in love with the island and has been living there longer than I have? Am I still more Dominican than this person?

That doesn't seem fair to me. In fact, it seems childish and absurd to divide people into these artificial boundaries. What if the world were our oyster? Where would *I* be? Where would *you* be? Whatever happened to cosmopolitanism? Could I ever forget where I came from?

This year I received the French citizenship and now my new passport tells me I'm French; better yet, European. Yet as much as I love French culture, and as good as my adoptive country has been to me, I know deep down with the same certainty I knew that I didn't belong on the island, that I will never stop explaining to people that I am Dominican. Somehow they recognize *mi alma caribeña.*

I guess Milan Kundera was right when he wrote that the "*…brevity of our life, […] allows us too little time to become attached to some other country, to other countries, to other languages.*" I would say we don't live long enough to get rid of the place we were born; nor do we live long enough to get fully attached to the place we want to belong to.

***

Lo más difícil es decirse a una misma que sí, que una puede;
es pararse e irse volando,
sin mirar hacia atrás.
Lo más difícil no es hablar en otro idioma:
es pensar en otro idioma,
es sentir en otro idioma,
es vivir en otro idioma,
es reír en otro idioma.
Cuando <<ja, ja, ja>> se convierte en asombro
con la dislexia y con cada chiste
que entiendes es más un <<ah, ah, ah entiendo>>,
que una carcajada sincera.
Lo más difícil no es mi cabello negro
o mi piel morena.
Lo más difícil es dudar de dónde vengo,
cuando otros no saben qué hacer conmigo,
ni con mi acento.
Lo más difícil no es estar lejos,
es estar cerca de gente que nunca te llamarán suya.
Lo más difícil no es llorar,
es creer que el llanto te hace menos fuerte,
menos valiente, menos gente.
Lo más difícil no son los silencios,
son las palabras vacías, sin sentimiento.
Lo más difícil no son los nuevos sonidos,
es aceptar cómo reverberan en tu cuerpo.
Lo más difícil no es ser de aquí sin estar allá.
Lo más difícil es estar aquí sin ser de allá.
Lo más difícil no es que te escuchen y no entiendan,
es que te vean y no te …

NI DE AQUÍ, NI DE ALLÁ

Lo más difícil no es querer los nuevos lugares.
Lo más difícil es olvidar los viejos.

During colonial times, the only condition to be considered *español* was to be white (pure-blood), regardless of the place of birth (Spain or the colonies)(this is improper english). This idea has permeated Latin American culture, and to this day, light-skin upper class Dominicans will brag about their immediate Spanish ancestry. In fact, in 2009, a modification to *La Ley de Memoria Histórica* in Spain allowed the grand-children of Spanish emigrants to apply for Spanish citizenship for a limited period of time.
[2] To be obscenely rich. *Cuarto* was the name of a now obsolete coin, used by Spain and its colonies during centuries XIV-XIX.
[3] Read as Pucamaima. PUCMM is the acronym for the Pontificia Universidad Católica Madre y Maestra, a catholic private university founded in 1962. Its main campus is located in Santiago de los Caballeros, with two smaller campuses in Santo Domingo and Puerto Plata.
[4] A car used for public transportation. It has a predetermined route and can take up to six passengers at a time, crammed in like sardines, excluding the driver. It's more or less the Dominican version of UberPool. The name *concho* derives from *Concho Primo*, a political fictional character created by Bienvenido Gimbernard, based on the Dominican *campesino*. During Trujillo's dictatorship, the first Chevrolet cars were imported onto the island, and somebody offered to use some of those cars to transport people on a predetermined route. To promote this new service amongst the poor population, Bienvenido Gimbernard himself suggested they call them *carro de Concho Primo*, which was shortened to *carro de concho*, thus *concho*.
[5] Many Dominicans living on the island will use the expression "los países" in plural, to refer to the United States or any other country where the Dominican diaspora has immigrated to.
[6] A popular slogan for *a casa de cambio* (exchange agency), claiming to change the remittances people received in American dollars to Dominican pesos, faster than it would take someone to say the word *berenjena* (eggplant in Spanish). The slogan then entered into popular culture as *very fast*.
[7] Dominicanismo for a 4x4 Jeep.
[8] Know-it-alls, people that believe they know everything about everything even if they have never heard about or studied about the matter before; It is a neologism, formed with the word "*todo*" (all or everything) and the suffix "*'logo,'* which is used in Spanish to designate a person who studies or has knowledge of a particular kind of science.
[9] Term used in the Dominican Republic and Puerto Rico meaning spinster.
[10] *El manda más* or the person with the highest rank, power or knowledge in a place. *Papaupa* was the name of a monkey that lived and dominated the zoo on the islet of La Matica, 35 km away from Santo Domingo.

135

El salón - Vanessa Chica Ferreira

Todos los domingos,
judged by the tight fitting pants, high heel wearing
dominicanas del salón

Siempre hablando de una dieta
o de la vecina
que está tan gorda.

As I sit roll heavy in their chair,
stuck between
their blah blah blahs,
and their understanding of my dominican hair.
Ahí es que nos entendemos.

This is where we meet,
between strands of hair,
between consejos;
*"Mezcla una cebolla con ron y póntelo en el pelo para que
se ponga fuerte.*
*Tómate un vaso de agua antes de comer para que te llenes y no comas
tanto."*

I just came to get my hair done,
paren de hablar.
"¿Tú eres dominicana?
No pareces."

No Somos Americanos - Joely Liriano

Its 1996 in Prince George's County, Maryland,
oh so many miles away from Haina & Cotui!
Trips to the Americana grocery in Cheverly
to get plátanos, shades of green & yellow

Waking up to *Intentalo tú* and opening gifts
not a minute before midnight on Noche Buena

Being called mixed in elementary school,
they never even knew my parents spoke
Spanish
At that time, we were only taught of mexicanos
and boricuas

"Cumpleaños feliz te deseamos a ti" sung right
after "how old are youuuu"

Fruit bowls and beautiful brown skin women are
the consistent theme in the paintings on our wall
reminds me of the tubi' and hairnets that
frequent the back of a motorcycle

Our flags hang in many places around the house
or on our car keys
to remind us we are never all here nor there

but our Caribeño pride carries in the form of
confidence, by the way we tell our stories

The heightened volume in our voices
might alarm the unfamiliar
it's not aggression, it's the sound of comforting words
settled in passionate statements

We may adapt to survive, pero nosotros no somos americanos.

¿Y tú?- Gerardo Carmen

-¿Tú eres Dominicana?
-! Sí!
-¿Y de qué parte?
-¡De la capital!
-¿Oh sí, y de qué parte? ...

Long extended pause...

-No sé... ¡Por Mega Centro!

In all honesty, it almost impairs my judgment having to come up with a legitimate answer; not because I am not Dominican, but because to many, I am not Dominican enough.

"Oh muchacha, pero tú eres americana" is always what comes next in response to me not being able to precisely identify the neighborhood from which my parents came from. Ugh! One wrong answer and you become someone else, a foreigner. Mucho peor, una americana. Well, I grew up eating plátanos, arroz con espaguetis, salchichón y bacalao, so, what's the problem?

I remember Juan Luis Guerra lulling me to sleep on Saturday nights, when my mom and dad were still together. I remember the pep in my step on Sunday mornings, awaiting the queso frito. Nah! Fuck that! ¡Yo soy dominicana! I know too much about my family's plight. I am fully aware of my country's fight against the injustices that have plagued it since my arrival in Nueva York. I have spent too many summers on an American Airlines flight for you to strip me of what I know I rightfully deserve to be called.

NI DE AQUÍ, NI DE ALLÁ

Don't get me wrong, I love being an American. My family's roots have also been welded into the foundations of many NYC apartments. In each and every one of them, we played la güira, made habichuela con dulce, have had hora santas for our departed, cried the tears of our ancestors and laughed at the giggles of our innocent children. Our mamás have told us not to look at cosas feas while pregnant, or to make sure we get to eat every pregnancy craving because if not, te sale el niño con un antojo en el cuerpo. I have closed many refrigerator doors after coming in from a hot summer day because let's be honest... "Nadie se quiere pasmar. "

I refuse to simply be called an American. I respect America because my parents immigrated here en búsqueda de un sueño, but you will not tell me what I am not! You will not tell me I am not a dominicana. It's in my blood, in the way I speak when I get upset, in the curves of my body, in the jokes I'm always proudly a victim of. It's in the rhythm of my feet. It is me. I am Dominican, call me anything you want, but do not tell me what I am not.

Americans have no problem acknowledging that I am Dominican. They use cute little names like immigrant, Latino, and Spanish girl. Sometimes they really go in and solidify their respect and admiration by calling me a spick. I'm guessing it's because when they see me, they feel like you do. They, too, see a foreigner, and they fear the unknown. To Americans, I am Dominican. To Dominicans I am an American. There must be a place where I fit in; a word that describes everything that I am because I am plenty. No me pondré límites because I know that like me, there are many.

We are infinite in our experiences, proud of our ancestors, and never give up hope that one day we won't be asked, "¿y tú?" Porque sinceramente, estoy cansada of the boxes we continuously have to check off. I am tired of having to prove my identity in not one but two idiomas ¿Y tú?

El ritmo de mi vida - Dafny Sánchez

Mi piel Canela
like the Sun,
Just bathed in doesn't fit
in both worlds
My hips sway to the rhythm…
the rhythm of my ancestors
but my lifestyle is running
on congested trains,
the smell of urine
and restless nights
"Cuando piso tierra dominicana,"
all those New York Blues
wash away
mi flor de mantequilla
in my hair,
gives me La llave de entrada,
to home
¡Soy tropical, soy el Caribe!
Soy el arroz y la habichuela,
que mi abuela cooks at noon.
Y el King Label that mi abuelo
dances to at night
as the sun,
the music and the palm trees
take over my being,
I realize that what I call home
might not always be home.
I'm stuck in two different worlds
where I don't know where I fit best
My mind is in the city,
but my soul is on that Island
which receives me with open arms
every time.
¡Soy dominicana!

To many I am not an island girl.
"Eta' e' la gringuita,"
but, No!

NI DE AQUÍ, NI DE ALLÁ

Even though my passport is blue,
I stay true
to where my calling is,
to where my soul is.
It's that guitar that plays
to the sound of the waves,
dancing to yellow sand,
united as one
under the sunset.
That's who I am
and that's who I will always be.

Quinces and Vegetables- Paloma Valenzuela
(Monologue from "The Pineapple Diaries"
Written for the Character of Lorismey)

I decided to become a vegetarian before my fiesta de Quinceañera, and let me tell you, my parents were not having it.

I sat my parents down and I told them some shit that a 15-year-old like me would say: "I am a woman now. I want my life decisions to be respected." It went something like that, while I probably tapped my index finger on the table with a stern face.

I was always an animal lover. I sympathized with the cows when I went to visit Tío's farm in Los Jobos. The rows of hanging chivos in Manoguayabo always made me cry, and I always dreamed of having a pet duck like in the Selena movie.

Anyways, I always wanted to be a vegetarian, but in my house, you ate what you were served.

But I figured, *I'm turning 15, I'm gonna be a woman now.* At 15, being a woman to me didn't mean wearing heels or being allowed to wear acrylic nails. Being a woman meant being my own person and making my own decisions. That was when I decided to commit to becoming a vegetarian, and to make that decision known.

For my quince, I wanted to create a completely vegetarian buffet! I wanted Dominican dishes with tofu guisado and quipes filled with cheese; delicious salads and moro with brown rice; habichuelas sans pork fat. Batatas everywhere! Batata postres, batata frita, batatas horneadas! It

142

was going to be healthy, delicious and animal free. People were going to walk out of my Quince like, "Oh yeah! I can do vegetarian!"

My parents were not supportive of my idea. "¡Oh oh! Pero, ¿tú quiere' que la gente pase hambre?" They didn't understand. They disregarded my decision, considering the declaration an inevitable teenage "gringa phase".

The day of my Quince, they bought a big lechón without my consent. They bought a MASSIVE lechón and put it right smack in the middle of the buffet. Surrounding the lechón were pastelitos, empanadas de pollo, quipes con carne de res, bistec, roast chicken, rice with bits of bacon in them, and a Caesar salad. I didn't check, but I wouldn't be surprised if the salad had hidden bacon in it, too, just to spite me. I was mortified.

During my dance with Papá, I couldn't stop staring at that pig. It stared at me, mouth agape, bright, red, and shiny. After dancing in those not-at-all-broken-into-yet heels, I was dying to put my flats back on so that I could run the hell out of there, away from that damn pig and away from my stupid party.

I was so pissed. I was pissed at my parents. At one point in the night, I burst into tears right where everyone could see me sitting on my big, white throne. I ran off to the bathroom, hoping there was a window I would be able to escape out of. There wasn't.

For the moment, the bathroom was escape enough. I looked at myself in the mirror, ringlet curls all crunchie and shit. My dress was lilac, with a layer of tulle and little glittering things all over the bust. I had make-up caked all over my face. Then I realized that... my parents didn't know who I was.

To them, that lechón was a symbol of their love for me. How would anyone know how much they loved me if they didn't throw me a lavish Quince, or put that expensive lechón on display? Yet all I wanted was a vegetarian feast. That's all.

I was able to come to terms with the reality that it wasn't my fantasy, it was theirs. There was no way I was ever going to fit in at a party like this, but they never considered other options. They had a daughter and their daughter had to have a Quince—the Quince of their dreams. They never considered the possibility that their daughter might not want any of it. Therefore, the tradition of misunderstanding on both ends lives on. I was their little girl. I was there for them. How would anyone know how much I loved my parents if I didn't come out in this puffy lilac dress and smile for the pictures? I told myself to suck it up, wiped the smudges of mascara off my reluctant face with the inside of my palms, and decided to go back outside.

When I opened the bathroom door, I was met with semi-remorseful, semi-confused looks on both my parent's faces. Papi was holding a box of cheese pizza from Bella Luna in his hands. They offered it to me and we didn't say a word. I just ran into their arms and felt thankful for the gesture. Maybe whatever was going on in the other room was some sort of built fantasy, a symbol of my rite of passage. It wasn't real to me. That moment with my parents in the bathroom hallway seemed like the real rite of passage.

The moment when your parents realize you are your own person. That moment you realize that no matter what, they're going to be there for you.

Mi greña - Sarah M. Bautista Suzaña

Me levanto con mi pelo vuelto un buen tollo,
pero libre, feliz, no está envuelto en un tubi
ni hay una gomita restringiendo la belleza
de sus hebras crespas y finas a la vez.
Mientras tanto, La Mega toca
las bachatas clásicas de mi madre;
cuales estaban en apogeo cuando ella lucía un pelo corto y alborotado.
Ella baila, limpia y cocina complaciendo como siempre esa doctrina
aprendida,
su pelo ya no luce igual.

Mi greña, mis rastas, un recuerdo constante de que las cosas no son como
antes.
Mis tatuajes algo de criminal.
Mis preguntas cuestionando.
¿Por qué los hombres comen primero?
¿Por qué siempre hay que mejorar la raza?
¿Por qué lo superficial es tan importante?
Mi pelo.

Mi pelo en la isla es una representación constante de lo que no soy;
Alisado, queratina, extensiones.
Mientras, tú eres aire libre, fresco, alegre,
con tus labios siempre pegados a una presidente verde como un alagarto

y tus manos en los blancos del domino y en la banca;
La Nacional, Quiniela Pale, Gana Más.
Mi pelo sumiso,
siempre duro, siempre feo.
He terminado con los días en que los asfixiaba en rolos para aparentar
decente, sensual, manejable.

Mi pelo ya no lleva rolos,
ya no se queda lacio,
no luce como todos los demás.
Me dicen:
—Wao, es diferente.
—Wao, ¿hasta cuándo te lo vas a dejar?

NI DE AQUÍ, NI DE ALLÁ

Aquí y ahora no saben qué pensar.
—¿Será hispana? ¿Hablará español?

—¿Qué es eso que tiene en la cabeza?
—Parece jamaiquina.

Mi pelo ya es libre de crecer,
ya no le importa ser definido,
ser limitado o ser uno entre todos.
Aún así, en este continente con millones de personas
de diferente razas y culturas
solo es a mi pelo al que miran.
—Se parece a Snoop Dog.
—Se parece a Bob Marley.
Mi pelo como yo, ni de aquí ni de allá.

Cornflakes and Plantains- Diely Pichardo

I first realized how powerful the United States was around the time my two front teeth came back in. A new, long-limbed student glided into our classroom at my elementary school in Salcedo, D.R. He was a "Dominican York" kid—the son of Dominicans living in New York. Another classmate whispered in my ear, "See how big he is? Americans are stronger and smarter than us because we grow up eating plantains and they grow up *eating conflé.*"

Back then, cornflakes were cost-prohibitive in the Dominican Republic, except for rich families. Plantains, rice, and beans were the base of our diets. Everybody "knew" that plantains contained a substance that made you dumb—yet the people making these claims didn't stop eating them. A simple glance at the side of a Frosted Flakes box would reveal the extensive list of vitamins the cereal contained—subtypes of B vitamins I didn't even know existed back then. If the list of nutrients didn't sell it, the ads with the Tiger would. Anyone who wanted their sports team to win had to eat Kellogg's Frosted Flakes. No wonder people from the US always won the Olympics while the D.R. rarely ever won anything. American athletes had Frosted Flakes for breakfast.

I tease David, my American-born, over six-foot-tall husband all the time about it (I would say my "gringo" husband, but he hates that word). "Of course you are taller and stronger than me," I tell him. "That's because *you grew up eating cornflakes.*"

I've been an official American now for almost a decade and living in the US for two—yet old habits are hard to break. I'm far from feeling like the "real American" David is. It's not about my DNA, my tanned skin, or my accent. It's about an intangible sense of privilege and pride

147

that had been unknown to me, until I heard the words "pursuit of happiness." I burst into tears the first time I grasped those words. I was studying for my naturalization exam. I had just left my then-husband after years of mistreatment, and still struggled with guilt of "giving up on him" and asking for a divorce. It was mind-blowing to think that in this country, seeking out my own happiness was not an act of selfishness but a *constitutional right.*

Even as a little girl, I knew what the word "American" meant. It meant: Be careful. This guy may look harmless, with his red-burnt skin, his goofy shorts, and his tendency to overpay, but if you lay a finger on him, he'll go to his consulate, summon the US Army, and you'll pay with your blood. In summary: *Don't mess with this one, someone has his back.*

What a wonderful and enviable thing to imagine! The Dominican government had NOBODY's back. Are you kidding me? I grew up scared of policemen because everyone knew they were the first suspects when a crime had occurred. After a lifetime of tasting presidential corruption and government abuse, my naturalization felt as though I were a battered child who had been rescued from a violent home, and brought to live with rich, adoptive parents. I felt grateful, cautious, and *very out of place.* I had to overcome decades of belonging to the oppressed group and prove I deserved my membership to this new family—this exclusive club of *The Winners of History.*

I must clarify that my husband David is not an average American. He has traveled extensively and acquired cosmopolitan tastes. (Proof of that? He married me!) Still, he is the best exponent of American ideals. I call it "the cornflakes personality." Other experts call it "the syndrome of growing up hearing that your country put people on the moon," or "the syndrome of *we have more missiles than all of you.*"

1- The Cornflakes Personality is pure *Self-Confidence.*

Once, I bought a TV. Right after unboxing it, I found a crack in the screen. The idea of having to return it to the store made my insides twist with anxiety. My hands trembled as I repacked it in its box. What if they didn't believe me when I said that it was already cracked? What if they said, "*you* broke it and now you're trying to make us refund you. Shame on you!" To make things worse, I couldn't find the receipt. I was sure the store would refuse to give me credit or an exchange, even if I brought the credit card I used to buy it.

My palms were sweaty against the steering wheel as I drove to Wal-Mart. I felt nauseous as I waited in line at customer service, listening to the dinging of cashier registers and the murmur of busy shoppers. I couldn't make eye contact with the clerk as I explained the situation. I expected her at any moment to scold me, or to at least interrogate me. "Can you prove you didn't do something to mess it up, drop it on the floor or hit it with a baseball bat?" Luckily, she didn't ask any of those questions and the exchange went smoothly.

My husband, David, on the other hand, has no problem with making returns or exchanges. Once, he bought a microwave that ended up being the wrong size for the space in our kitchen. He had already thrown away the packing materials, and before we could prevent it, one of our kids had used the microwave to reheat lasagna, coating its insides with marinara sauce.

David didn't even blink. He showed up to the store with no receipt, no box, and no packing materials. Calmly, he laid the dirty marinara-stained microwave on the customer service counter and demanded his money back—*and succeeded*. He does things like that all the time. Once, he didn't like the produce he bought. A week later, he returned to the grocery store, helped himself to a bag of tomatoes, and politely told the cashier that "the last tomatoes [he] bought here were overripe, so [he's] taking these in exchange, and they should be free of charge." He did that with no receipt, no proof, and without bringing back the spoiled tomatoes and nobody questioned him. He walked out of the store with free goods and an apology from the store manager.

I couldn't do that in a million years. Just like dogs can smell fear, they'd assume I'm lying even if I'm not, just by my shaking. David, with all his cornflake personality radiance, possesses a self-assurance that hypnotizes people. I have a theory that that's how he got me to give our relationship a chance—but that's another story.

2- The Cornflakes personality *doesn't tolerate mistreatment.*

David is so deeply convinced of his own value, he doesn't waste energy explaining it to people. If someone is being rude or inattentive to him, he just walks away. More than an (one?) ex-girlfriend found out the hard way. One woman dared to say, "it's me or the cat," never really expected him to choose the feline. David doesn't do well with ultimatums.

In contrast, I spent a decade of my life in an oppressive marriage. Still carrying the Plantain Mentality, I accepted it as natural that my Dominican ex-husband claimed absolute control of my life. I resigned to his pathological jealousy that isolated me from my friends for years. I internalized his constant comments, which I now understand were meant to crush my self-esteem so I'd never leave him. I submitted to double standards and contributed all the childcare, cooking, and cleaning, even if both of us worked the exact same hours as medical residents.

I needed years of therapy before I gathered the strength to walk away from him and his mistreatment. Still, after all that, it took reading about "the pursuit of happiness" before I forgave myself for it and moved on.

3- The Cornflakes Personality is *efficient and reliable.*

David is reliable like the sun and expects reliability from other people. I'm the woman who's always expecting everyone to fail. Having grown up in a place where, from water to electricity, you could never count on a service, I always assumed services simply don't work. I drive to the post office and refuse to leave stamped mail in the mailbox because I still can't believe that a mailman will really come and get it. I'm still surprised each time the USPS comes through and delivers my mail without losing it.

David is also compulsively punctual and has a low tolerance for tardy people. I am too, and that's one of the reasons why I always felt like a misfit in the DR, where people proudly said that "Dominican time" is two hours later than what was stamped on every invitation. Once, after eleven years of living in the US, I returned to my Dominican Alma Mater, PUCMM, to speak at a Medical Conference. My lecture was scheduled for 9:00 a.m. It was 11:00 a.m. and the previous speaker was still going. I couldn't believe no one else considered that disrespectful. "Relax, this is normal," another doctor next to me said. "You've become such an American!"

The heartbreaking realization hurt. He was right; I was a foreigner in my own country. That day, I made the decision to apply for American citizenship.

Still, there is something else to being an American, beyond self-confidence, reliability, and punctuality. It's something difficult to explain; self-assurance above and beyond anything I've ever been able to achieve. The word had eluded me, but it hit me recently: *Entitlement.*

I was amazed to realize that there was no Spanish equivalent for the world *Entitlement.* Google translates it to "derecho," which actually translates to "right," or "privilegio," privilege." However, the word "entitlement" has an extra ring—A ring that can sometimes come across as arrogance. The rest of the time it sounds more like "good things are not just a right and a privilege. *I deserve them.*"

That is the difference between Plantain-Me and Cornflakes-David. He cruises through life assuming that when things don't go his way, that that's the exception to the rule and not the norm. That gives him an edge on taking risks, and he gets away with more in life than I do. He expects good outcomes, and most of the time the world says, "Amen."

There is such a thing as the power of the mind. I'm convinced that the handyman will not show up—and he doesn't. I'm convinced that my airline will mess up my seat—and they do. I'm convinced that all other authors in the world (those who had the privilege of growing up eating cornflakes) will have an advantage over me, and my efforts for promotion will be in vain—and more often than not, the world says, "Amen."

I can already hear other cornflakes science scholars refuting my theories. "You didn't describe the American Archetype, you described the *White-Male Syndrome!*" I can also see my Dominican relatives rolling their eyes and saying, "Why are you praising entitlement? It's the same quality that has allowed the US to invade other countries and help themselves to everyone else's natural resources." I can even add that there are many advantages to growing up without entitlement: You're more likely to appreciate the little things you do get.

Yes, having too much of a good thing becomes a bad thing; but having zero of it becomes worse. The entitlement I advocate for is not about arrogance; it's about the American spirit that says, "I give respect, so I deserve respect."

Dominicans have a wonderful ability to be happy with little, and that has enriched my capacity for joy throughout my life. At the same time, that virtue becomes a burden if it stops us from pursuing a better life. A decade ago, I summoned the power of the American Archetype. I decided to value myself enough to fight for my happiness, and I chose to believe that I deserve good things in my life. I left an oppressive husband.

Pursuing happiness paid off. Today, I'm married to someone who treats me like an equal—more than an equal. My beloved Yankee, David, treats me like a *princess*. I remind myself about that whenever I have to return something to the store, or launch a new book, or make a career decision. It's fine. Someone has my back. I've taken risks before, and those proved worth it.

It's okay to believe we deserve more. It's okay, even advisable, to bring a little more cornflak into our lives.

SOY/I AM - Viusmy Damian

Soy cálida, sonriente,
mi luz resembla el sol
en días de playa...
Provengo de un país caribeño,
de gente humilde de corazón,
gente amable y trabajadora,
que se levanta con el cántico de los gallos,
con el tumulto de los vendedores y del tráfico en la ciudad...
Soy de donde las palmeras y las rosas de Bayahíbe
decoran toda Quisqueya embelleciendo cada rincón...

Soy una muñeca sin cara
que representa el origen de nuestra etnicidad.
Sin embargo, mi piel solo refleja una pieza del rompecabezas
de una isla rica impregnada por historias de felicidad y amarguras,
del sin sabor de un horizonte el cual cautiva por su belleza natural,
pero el cual oculta las desigualdades de un pueblo que vive al día....

Soy Dominicana...

Soy Dominicana...

Soy una muñeca sin cara, mi piel es constituida de varios tonos...

Soy de tez blanca, morena, negra, trigueña...

Soy de cabellos crespos, rizos, lacios...

I am from where I was born.
I am from where I am right now.
I am from all the places that I have been.
I am from all the places that I will be.
But above all, I am that place gathering
Selected, subjective poetry
on my own trail.

Comrade, Bliss ain't playing, Josefina Báez

CONTRIBUTORS

BREMDA ACOSTA is a poet and a sociologist from San Cristobal, Dominican Republic. She found her love for writing at the age of 13, having lived in New York City for a year and also just having realized that her world would always exist between Spanish, her mother tongue, and English, the language of her newfound home. Most of her poems explore life between here and there, or as Josefina Baez defines it, El Nie. Bremda received a bachelor's degree in Global Public Health and Sociology from NYU. Currently, she is pursuing a PhD degree in Sociology at Syracuse University, where she intends to study black liberation movements in the Caribbean, and the efforts of female-led organizations in the Dominican Republic that fight for women's political and reproductive rights.

PAMELA MICHELLE BALBUENA DE GARDOS was born on September 4th, 1985 in Santo Domingo, Dominican Republic. She is the oldest out of 3 kids. Pamela completed her elementary and secondary school years at Santa Teresa School. Later, after watching her parents run a retail business store, she started her major in business administration. While in college, she met professional table tennis player, Robert Gardos, who she later married. Pamela studied in Europe and graduated with a degree in diplomatic relations. She's currently a mom of three kids: Alejandro (2010), Alicia (2015), and Emma (2020). Pamela discovered her passion for writing in high school and it has remained an important part of her life since then as she faces it with passion and humbleness.

ARMANDO BATISTA is a poet, performing artist, and educator. He hails from Washington Heights, NY and is the son of Dominican immigrants. He is an artist driven by the creative process, personal mythology, and socially conscious themes. In his writing, Armando explores themes such as identity, race, urban and cultural mythology, 80's nostalgia, the extraordinary every-day, and love in all its complexities. His poetry can present as the word on the page, abstract ideas remixed into image, or a live multi-media performance; Storytelling is boundless and uses varying forms to shape its sharing. Armando has an MFA in Writing from Vermont College of Fine Arts and a BA in Theater from Temple University. His poetry has appeared in the Manhattan Times and Cracken, an international literary magazine, published in the Caribbean. He is currently working on a poetic manuscript titled RoaDMaN, which he hopes to publish in 2021.

SARAH BAUTISTA describes herself as a young Latinx writer that is trying to add to the world through her work. She was born in the United States but describes herself as being culturally Dominican. Sarah was raised in the South Bronx and had the privilege of attending college out of state. She studied abroad in Mendoza, Argentina while completing her undergraduate degree, earning a Spanish Literature degree. She is an outgoing introvert that is continuously trying to be the best version of herself. Her ultimate goal is to help break generational traumas within herself and the community, while spreading openness and compassion.

GISSELLE BELIA is a public administrator and self taught writer. She wrote her first series of poems when she was 12 years old in the Dominican Republic. She graduated from Baruch College with a degree in Public Affairs and a minor in English. She draws inspiration for her poems from her family, social justice, and self love. Gisselle Belia is passionate about food access and inequality in poor neighborhoods, and discrimination in the Dominican Republic. Ms. Belia dreams of becoming a full time writer. She resides in NYC with her family.

GABRIELA BLANCO BOBEA was born in Santo Domingo, Dominican Republic. Raised by her grandmother in the community of Alma Rosa. She harnessed an early interest and natural talent for poetry and storytelling. By fifteen, her work had been published in national newspapers El Listín Diario and Hoy. Gabriela's life in the Dominican diaspora began when she and her mother moved to New York City as undocumented immigrants in the 1990s. The road to and from home over the years was a winding one, eventually leading her to a degree in Creative Writing and Neurolinguistics from one of the most notable liberal arts programs in the United States. Her thesis, Espejismos por Oro (Mirrages for Gold), was an investigative narrative centered around the consequences of corporate tourism in Dominican coastal communities, as told through interviews conducted with hotel and resort employees. She was the winner of The Annual Five-College "WORD!" Festival for her play, *Gallo*.
Currently, Gabriela lives in New York City where she explores the fluid course of personal identity and resilience through her writing and photography. She writes fluently in Spanish, English, and French. Her upcoming collection of poems navigates the internal and external
dialogues of Caribbean womanhood in the global sphere.

EMANUEL CABREJA is a Domini-Rican man who was born and raised in West Harlem, New York, where he developed and continues to nurture his fascination with multiculturalism, including his own Latinidad and Afro-Caribbean heritage. As a student of life with a penchant for people, society and the humanities, he rediscovered poetry writing as a tool for managing depression and anxiety, specifically as it relates to personal and vicarious trauma, using it to face the man in the mirror daily. Cabreja has a BA from The City College of New York (CUNY) in psychology and an MSW from the Silberman School of Social Work at Hunter College (CUNY). He is knowledgeable about the brain and mind, and is deeply interested in history, spirituality, and philosophy. You can find his writing on online platforms such as Mirakee, Quora, and Instagram, where he hopes to inspire others to feel and think deeply. He is slowly working on self-publishing a book of poetry and is considering pursuing other writing genres, including short stories, plays, and blogs. For more information or writing samples, you can reach him at mr.sensitivemacho@gmail.com.

ROXANA CALDERÓN is a writer and editor born in Brooklyn, New York and raised in the Dominican Republic. She emerges from a new generation of young Latin writers in the United States. After more than 10 years of providing support to students in underserved areas of New York, Calderon opted to dive into unknown waters and wrote her first book, "La Casa de las Maletas" (2019, NYC). She possesses an intrinsic ability to describe through her writing what often seems irrational to the brain and emotional to the heart. In her book, Roxana uses her original voice to speak about the things nobody dares to. Calderón has been featured in lagaleriamag.com (Un Verano en Nueba Yol' 2019), dominicanwriters.com (Las Hijas de Machepa 2019), and spanglishvoces.com (El Componente & Confesión a un desconocido 2020). She has participated in the anthologies from the Americas Poetry Festival of New York, Multilingual Anthology (Just Listen/Solo Escucha 2019), and in the Latin American anthology, "El vuelo más largo," published by Angeles del Papel Editores, in Perú (years?). Roxana is the Managing Editor of digital literary magazine, *Spanglish Voces,* and a collaborator of the Dominican Writers Organization. Her work was recently highlighted in two of the most important newspapers in the Dominican Republic: Diario Libre and Listín Diario. Roxana Calderón lives in New York and works as a Senior Program Director in Washington Heights, overseeing various educational programs at a local not for profit organization.

AILA SHAI CASTANE is a writer, thinker, healer, and dancer whose work reflects her Afro- Dominican and Afro-Cuban roots, as well as her Spanglish tongue. She believes in the potency of movement, words, and storytelling as a tool for healing, remembering, and archiving. Born in Washington Heights, New York and raised in the suburbs of Virginia Beach, Virginia, Aila Shai often writes about her afro-latinidad and the duality of the worlds that she navigates as both a Latina and as a Black American, and how those worlds frame her experience in the diaspora. Aila Shai holds a BA in Mass Communications from Virginia Commonwealth University, with double minors in African American Studies and Gender, Sexuality and Women's Studies. Her work has been published in several volumes of *Amendment*, a progressive literature and art journal produced by Virginia Commonwealth University students, that provides a platform to promote equality, tolerance, and social progression through artistic expression. This is her first published piece outside of the university press.

YOSELI CASTILLO FUERTES was born in the Dominican Republic in 1972 and migrated to the United States at 16. She holds a BA in Psychology and an MA in Spanish Literature. She is a bilingual-afro-dominican-latina-lesbian-poet-activist-teacher-aunt. She is a Cave Canem alumni. Her poems and short stories have appeared in various anthologies and online magazines in New York, Buenos Aires, Madrid and Santo Domingo. Her self-published poetry book, De eso sí se habla/Of That, I Speak, is on sale at cyoseli@yahoo.com. She is currently working on a short story collection and her second poetry book.

PAOLA CESPEDES is the daughter of Dominican immigrants, born and raised in New Jersey. She is a creative nonfiction writer and poet belonging to the Women's Poetry Workshop in Brooklyn and the Dominican Writers Association based in Washington Heights. Earning her BA in Communication Arts and Writing, her auto ethnography was presented at Eastern Communication Association (Pittsburgh, PA 2018) and later published in the Harvard Latinx literary magazine *Palabritas* (Cambridge, MA 2019). Her writing is a direct response to the erasure and misrepresentation of the stories and images of Afro-Latinx women and their exclusion from the media. Her writing explores sexuality, identity, gender roles, and internalized racism. Paola is currently reading through her library and cautiously writing her first collection of poetry.

YUBANY CHECO was born in Santiago, Dominican Republic. He graduated with a degree in management of Information Systems from the Stevens Institute of Technology, Telematics at Universidad Catolica Madre y Maestra and Electronics at Hesston College. He enrolled in creative and academic writing courses at Duke University, Taller Literario Narradores de Santo Domingo (TLNSD) and Asociación Dominicana de Ficción Especulativa (ADFE). He is a two-time winner of NaNoWriMo (2018, 2019). Yubany is the winner of the "De la idea al objeto"; contest organized by Taller Literario Narradores de Santo Domingo. first book, *Pequeñas Sombras Humanas* was published in 2018. He won third place in the Casa De Teatro International Short Story contest in 2018 and was
a finalist in the Alianza Cibaeña, Juan Bosch and Lauro Zabala short story contests in 2019. His published works can be found in digital magazines and anthologies such as the Winter Writing Contest for Short Fiction Break (2016), Minatura (2017), Móntame una escena del taller español Literautas (2016), en la antología Se nos fue poniendo viernes la tarde del Taller Literario Narradores de Santo Domingo (2017), First sellection of short stories especulative fiction of Asociación Dominicana de Ficción Especulativa (2019), antologies: 2020-SOS (2020) y Papeles de la pandemia for Letralia (2020). Anthologist of the award-winning short story book Sombreros para gatos (TLNSD) and for Galipotes y Robots (ADFE). He is also radio broadcaster and writer for taekwondo magazine MasTKD.

NI DE AQUÍ, NI DE ALLÁ

VIUSMY S. DAMIAN URENA is a multidisciplinary artist who writes poems and loves to make art. Her artwork focuses on raising awareness for the socio-political, environmental, cultural and ethnic issues affecting humanity. Viusmy works as a case manager for a social service organization in New Jersey. She is currently completing a master's degree in Mental Health Counseling with an Art Therapy specialization at Caldwell University.

JAROL FABIO was born in Santo Domingo, Dominican Republic and moved to New York at the age of 4. Jarol Fabio had, as he proclaims, the "honor" of growing up in Washington Heights and getting to experience the duality of Dominican living in NYC, like DR but with all four seasons. On one of his Santo Domingo layovers as a flight attendant, Jarol stopped by his abuela's house for a quick visit. His aunt greeted him and praised him for his aesthetic, claiming that Jarol had always been a "morenito lavado," a phrase he did not understand at the moment. The phrase means "clean brown (black)." He is a racial anomaly of class, if you will. This phrase led Jarol to interrogate the parallels of both societies, which he calls home. Through cunning humor and a knack for storytelling, Jarol takes the reader on a vibrant, and at times visceral journey as he recalls stories around identity, race, sexuality, mental health, and culture. Jarol holds a BA in International Trade & Marketing with a minor in French from the Fashion Institute of Technology in New York City. Jarol lives in Midtown, Manhattan with his French bulldog named Pancho.

ASTRID FERGUSON is a Dominican and Haitian certified life coach, author and poet. She was born in Dominican Republic, raised in New York and resides on the outskirts of Philly, PA. Her hope is to inspire women to quit playing small and embrace the transition of building the career and life of their dreams. Astrid has a bachelor's degree in Business Information Systems and a Masters in Business Administration. Aside from her writing, Astrid has built a career in the corporate pharmaceutical sector. Currently, she is focusing on building her life and career coaching business. When she is not working she is playing referee with her two boys and talking art with her husband, Jerel Ferguson. Her writing has been published by numerous small presses and online magazines such as *Alegria Magazine, Genre Urban Arts, She Will Speak Series, Spoken Black Girl, La Galeria Mag* and *Harness Magazine,* to name a few. She has also self-published two anthologies, *Molt* and *The Serpent's Rattle.*

JUDY FERNDANDEZ DIAZ is a Dominican woman who is proud of her African roots. She was born in the Bronx and raised both in Providence, RI and Santiago, Dominican Republic. As a first generation Dominican- American, she was raised bilingual and bicultural. Thus, many of her poems are in Spanglish. During her time in Santiago, she published two YA novels in Spanish. She is currently writing a middle grade fantasy (novel?) in English. Fernandez Diaz is a Human Resources executive with over 20 years of HR experience. She has a dual degree in Psychology and Human Services from Boston University. She also has a master's degree in Organizational Psychology from Columbia University. She is a member of the Society of Children's Book Writers and Illustrators and was selected as a Las Musas Books mentee for spring 2020. Judy currently resides in Tolleson, Arizona with her beautiful daughter.

VANESSA CHICA FERREIRA is an NYC educator, writer, poet, playwright and fat activist. She has been a featured poet at various events throughout New York City. She co-wrote and performed in a 3 woman play titled "Live Big Girl," which debuted December 2017 at The National Black Theatre. She is a former member of Machete Movement, a world music band featuring percussion and spoken word. Her poems can be found in "The Girl With The Smile" poetry chapbook, *The BX Files: Contemporary Poetry from the Bronx Anthology*, the Elkat Productions *Live Big Girl* poetry anthology, *The Abuela Stories Project*, *The Acentos Review Online*, and the Great Weather For Media anthology, *Escape Wheel*. Vanessa Chica believes there is strength in vulnerability and is getting stronger every day. For more information, please visit VanessaChica.com

MAYRENES FIGUEREO is a first generation Dominican-American born and raised in Jersey City, New Jersey. Later, she awkwardly blossomed in Suffolk, Virginia, where she resided during her teenage and young adult years. She attended Norfolk State University, an HBCU, and found herself on a study abroad trip to the Dominican Republic one summer.
On that trip, she re-learned to love her culture, her identity and herself. In 2014, she earned a Bachelor of Arts degree in English and a Bachelor of Arts degree in Psychology. She moved to New York to pursue a Master's Degree in School Counseling, graduating from New York University in 2016. She currently lives in Detroit, Michigan with her husband, and works as a school counselor. Her hope is to help empower Black and Brown kids to achieve far more than what society has set them up for.
Instagram @sinceramente_may -- Twitter @sinceramentemay

ALBERT GARCIA initiated his writing career with a publication in *The Atticus Review*. His first short-story, "A Child's Hood/A Childhood," focuses on themes of Hispanic identity, stereotypes, and anxiety. Albert also self-published a short-story collection titled *Nostalgia*, for which he wrote five stories in both English and Spanish. As a young Dominican writer, he uses his pen to represent his community. His writing style is vivid in color and rich with flavor. Albert has a BA from John Jay College in Sociology, with a minor in Anthropology. He is currently pursuing an MA at The City College of New York in the Study of the Americas with a focus on Dominican Studies. To find more of Albert's work, you can visit his online journal at albertgarciawrites.wordpress.com.

LOURDES A. GAUTIER is a poet and writer of short fiction and non-fiction. Born in Santo Domingo, Dominican Republic and raised in New York City, she earned a Master of Arts degree in Theatre and post graduate credits in a doctoral program at the City University of New York (CUNY), focusing on Latin American Theatre. She taught courses in acting and theatre history and criticism at CUNY, Drew University, and Jersey City State University. She taught language arts in a special grant funded program at Rutgers University, Newark campus. Her short story, "1952", was published in the *Acentos Review*. Her poems have appeared in *Cagibi Literary Review, Calliope, Dying Dahlia Review*, and in the *Silver Birch Press All About My Name, My Perfect Vacation, and Meta-morphosis* series, among others. She is also a contributor to the award winning anthology, *These Winter Months: The Late Orphan Project*. She has performed at the Inwood Local open mic night in New York City and participated in the inaugural Cagibi Writer's Retreat in Hudson County. She was a featured poet at Second Saturdays at Cyrus, hosted by Terri Muuss and Matt Pasca. Recently retired from a position as an administrator at Columbia University, she is working on a collection of poems and stories. Her writing focuses on the issues of identity as an Afro-Latina, the many faces of love, and saudade or anhelo, a longing for a place to call home.

GREISY GENAO (she/they) is a poet and filmmaker from Queens, NY. They hold a BA in English Writing and Film Studies. They're a multidisciplinary story teller, interested in capturing the mysticism and magic of the Dominican diaspora. In 2018, Greisy won a Fulbright U.S Student Researcher award to study the effects of Dominican folklore on diasporic Dominican cinema. While there, Greisy taught screenwriting and wrote and directed "Si Ardiera La Ciudad," their debut short film that is currently competing internationally. Greisy's poetry and film work can be found in the anthology, *Women of Eve's Garden, Ritmo Que Late* by the Dominican Writers Association, Sarah Lawrence College's *Lumina* Journal, and *La Galeria Magazine*. Their book, *Despierta*, can be found at the CUNY Dominican Studies Institute Library in New York and the Roy O. West Library at DePauw University, in Greencastle, Indiana. For more of their poetry, check out their personal IG account @grei_mg.

CARMEN GERARDO-RUBIO is an advocate and educator. Relentless and self determined, she attended CUNY for her undergrad and graduate education. Though both of her parents are immigrants from the Dominican Republic, her American roots are in Brooklyn, her birthplace—but both Queens and Long Island have witnessed her come much more into herself. There are a few people Carmen can't live without: her sons, Isaias and Nico, her husband, Amaury, and her pitbull, Jax. She loves words, jazz and a room flushed with natural light. Carmen writes to remind herself that words have power and are healing.

Through her connection with words, she will always find a way to assert her agency.

LORENA GERMÁN is a Dominican American writer who is a wife, mami, and educator in Austin, Texas. She teaches young people to be anti racist and supports teachers with the skills to do the same. Her writing has been featured by the Undertone Collective and in Ana Castillo's zine, "La Tolteca 2.0," among other publications. Lorena earned her Master of Arts from the Middlebury College Bread Loaf School of English. She is Co-Founder of #DisruptTexts as well as Co-Founder of the Multicultural Classroom. Her writing is a form of exhaling. She tries, she fights, she solves problems and heals, in and through writing. Follow her on Twitter @nenagerman.

ROBERTO GERMÁN is a Dominican-American native of Lawrence, Massachusetts. He supported the opening of Magnolia Montessori For All, Austin's first public Montessori school, serving as Director of Student Affairs and Services. He has also served as Assistant Principal at the Guilmette Middle School in Lawrence, MA and as Director of Multicultural Affairs and Community Development for seven years at St. John's Preparatory School in Danvers, MA. While there, he led the school in
fostering a culture that promoted social justice and equity. Mr. Germán is an alumnus of Andover Bread Loaf and an active member of the Bread Loaf Teacher Network. His role within ABL and with the BLTN is at the center of ABL's educational justice work within the public schools and youth and community organizations. When he was twenty years old, Roberto introduced and co-led a spoken word movement in the city of Lawrence that took the city by storm from 2001-2003. This movement became the beginning of a writing revolution that inspired young people in the city of Lawrence to find their voices through the arts, particularly spoken word poetry and rap. He accomplished this with his former performing arts group, the Soul Kaliber Movement, and by his ability to collaborate with diverse organizations and individuals. He holds a master's degree from Boston College's Lynch School of Education in Educational Administration and a Bachelor of Arts in English from Merrimack College. Currently, Roberto is the Middle School Director at Headwaters School in Austin, Texas.

QUIZAYRA GONZALEZ received her BFA in Multimedia from the University of the Arts and a master's degree in Design Studies from Parsons School of Design. Her writing and curatorial work focuses on identity formation and belonging. Quizayra's curatorial work includes *Futurographies: Cambodia, US, France* for the Shelia C. Johnson Design Center, and *Crafted Strangers* for the Center for Craft, Creativity, and Design. Currently, Quizayra leads a team of academic advisors who focus on supporting students and creating inclusive learning spaces. Her writing has been published in *La Galeria Magazine, the*

Latino Book Review Literary Magazine, Urban Omnibus, and Public Seminar. In the fall of 2020, Quizayra will begin a master's program in Education at Harvard Graduate School of Education.

ANA MARÍA GONZÁLEZ PUENTE was born in El Seibo, Dominican Republic. She currently resides in New York City. Her latest published novel, *Doña Tina* has been awarded first place for Best Popular Fiction – Spanish, and second place for Best Novel – Adventure or Drama – Spanish at the 2019 International Latino Book Awards. In 2015, *¡A estudiar, carajo!* was awarded first place for Best Latino Focused Fiction Book – Spanish at the International Latino Book Awards. In 2012, *Del suelo al cielo* obtained second place for Best Novel – Adventure or Drama – Spanish or Bilingual at the International Latino Book Awards. *The Divorce* is a translation of *Del suelo al cielo*.

YADIRA ILEANA GRULLÓN is a dedicated mother to she and her husband, Kristopher's greatest gifts, Keira and Bryce. She is dedicated to her parents (they all live under one roof together forever) who were born in the Dominican Republic, and her siblings, Ralph and Xavier. She is dedicated to her profession, working with some of the most prominent health and retirement funds in the country. She is dedicated to maintaining her Corona roots (she was born in Queens) and currently lives in Princeton Junction, NJ. She is dedicated to being a fit and healthy vegan. She is a dedicated volunteer Spanish-language translator, including for a non-profit organization. Grullón has a BS in Secondary English Education from New York University. She received a Certificate of Merit for Excellence in Playwriting from New York City Public Schools and an Honorable Mention in a poetry contest from the City University of New York.

YULISSA HIDALGO is a Dominican-American writer, educator, actress, and director. She was born and raised in Washington Heights. She attended public schools throughout Manhattan until she received a scholarship to Bucknell University, in Lewisburg, Pennsylvania. While enrolled, Yulissa studied Theater, Women & Gender Studies, and Creative Writing. In 2012, her poetry was first published in the school's literary magazine, *Fire and Ice*, and she was the recipient of the Julia Fonville Smithson Poetry Award. Upon graduation, she went on to pursue a graduate degree in arts and education at NYU Steinhardt. She has taught Theater and English for the past seven years. Currently, Yulissa teaches ninth grade writing in Rye, New York.

DANNY JIMENEZ is a man with roots in the Dominican Republic, Sub-Saharan Africa, and Spain. He was born and raised by a single mother in Inwood. His mission is to help the disenfranchised by improving their literacy and putting them in positions to help their neighborhood. Danny has a BA from John Jay College of Criminal Justice in English with an undeclared minor in

Latinx Literature. He is a member of Sigma Tau Delta, the International English Honors Society. He is an advocate of literacy and equality and his expertise lies in literature. He currently serves as a YA Librarian specializing in Teen Programming. His writing has been published on the Dominican Writers Association's website.

Poem: https://www.dominicanwriters.com/post/tell-me

Danny currently resides in The Bronx with his fiancee and three dogs: Dionysus aka Dio "The underage citizen,"Chloe "The Mayor," and Charlie, "The Public Advocate." He is an avid reader and a fan of the 007 series. Likes his drinks shaken, not stirred.

JOELY LIRIANO is a writer with roots in the Dominican Republic. She was born and raised in Prince George's County, MD. She began writing in her early childhood as a form of release and expression. Liriano released her first poetry book, *Letters I Never Sent: Thus Never Received* in September 2018. It is a collection of poems inspired by the
idea of writing letters to the closest people in her life without ever sending them.

WENDY MELLA CARREÑO is a dominican photographer, currently residing in New York City. A graduate of the New York Institute of Photography, her mission has always been to express herself and her longing for her native country through the work she does. Wendy is also a community contributor who strongly believes in social justice, which she advocates for through her art. She is also known as "OjoIntruso" (The Intruder Eye), which is the brand name of her photography business. Either through photography, videography or writing, Wendy has always sought to tell a story; her story and the stories of those around her. Wendy has spent years developing her craft and bringing her ideas to life. As an emerging writer, Wendy seeks to incorporate her passion for the visual arts into her writing, and to continue to share what she sees and feels through storytelling.

ASHANTI MUÑIZ is a first generation Dominican American, born and raised in Uptown, New York. She discovered her passion for language in the fourth grade, extending creative word play from poetry to typography. Ashanti has a Bachelor of Arts degree from Marymount Manhattan College in Graphic Design, with a minor in Creative Writing. She works as a freelance artist, selling works at local events and performing at poetry slams. Her works have been exhibited and shared within community events and at the Rio II Gallery in 2018, as well as the NYC Poetry Festival. Ashanti's mission is to show how the power of creativity can transform the world around us for the better and to remind her audience that when we create something from nothing, we have the freedom to create something of peace. Ashanti currently resides in Manhattan, New York.

LUZ OZORIA is a Dominican-American woman. She was born in Washington Heights and grew up, moving more times than she could count, between Dominican Republic, Long Island, and NYC. After years of being silenced by the weight of both her experiences and generational trauma, she found writing at a pivotal point in her life. Writing gives her an unconfined space to speak her truth, both liberating and saving her. Her mission is for her writing to be a reflection in which other brown girls can see themselves and their stories. She is writing for girls like her 12 year old self. She has no formal writing training, but hopes to begin an MFA soon in preparation for her first novel. For the past seven years, she has been a spoken word poet and performance art curator. She has been featured at places like Bowery Poetry Club, People's Music Network, El Puente, the LATEA Theater and various others. Luz currently resides in Long Island, New York.

VANESSA PARDO is a first-generation Latina-American. She was born and raised in Washington Heights. She is on a mission to break generational cycles and normalize creating your own lane. Vanessa has a Master of Science in Education with a concentration in School Psychology from Brooklyn College. In 2020, she parted ways with the NYC Department of Education after serving the public-school community as a Bilingual School Psychologist for over five years, in order to be present for her family and herself. Her writing has been published in *Hispanecdotes*. Vanessa currently resides in New Jersey.

MAYELYN PERDOMO SANTOS was born and raised in the Bronx by a mother from Cotui and a father from San Francisco de Macoris. She writes poems in Espanglish para recordad where she's from. Perdomo Santos holds a Bachelor of Arts from Hunter College in English, with a focus in teaching literature for adolescent education. She is passionate about creating community through the arts and educating young people. She has worked as a teaching artist and tutor all across New York City. Her performance credits include Public Works Shakespeare in The Park and 54 Below. Most recently, she made her playwriting and directorial debut with Showdogs' Playwrights Collective. Follow her for more on Instagram @mayelyn.ps.

DR. DIELY PICHARDO-JOHANSSON is a Board Certified oncologist, Life Coach and author living in Florida. She's published eight novels, including the critically-acclaimed *Faith is Fearless: Normal is Overrated*. She's a Summa Cum Laude graduate from PUCMM in the Dominican Republic, where she received her medical degree. She obtained her hematology-oncology specialization from Northwestern University in Chicago, and her internal medicine training from Wayne State University in Detroit. She lives in Melbourne Beach, Florida with her soulmate-husband and her four children, including twins and a child with special needs. As a firm believer in love and the healing power of laughter, she only writes positive stories that are uplifting to

165

the heart. Her romance specialty is the "connection of the minds and souls, more than only the bodies." Her mystery specialty is "how to murder someone and ensure a negative autopsy." You can learn more about her work at her Author's website: https://pichardo-johansson-md.com/

AGUEDA PIZARRO was born and raised in Santo Domingo. She does not remember the year. Her work has been published in: *Antología de Comunidad Poética RD Generación XXI (2019)*; *Palabritas Magazine Spring Issue (2019)*; *Antología Digital Boliviana Microcuentos de terror* *"En Tiempos de Coronavirus" (2020)*. She was the second place winner of the Mujeres Inspiradoras contest in 2018. She lives to write about it and works to buy books. @aguedalandia

MARÍA LIGIA RIVAS is a Dominican-born Marketing Associate living in Marseille, France. She has a double master's degree in Media Law from Aix-Marseille University and International Business from Lumière Lyon 2 University, both located in France. She has been writing as a hobby since she was a child, but this is the first time she is submittings her work for publication. You can follow her on Instagram @ml_rvs.

INES P. RIVERA PROSDOCIMI is a poet, comparatist, and Caribbeanist. Her poetry collection, *Love Letter to an Afterlife* (Black Lawrence Press, 2018), was a finalist for the 2019 International Latino Book Awards (Best Poetry Book) and the 2019 Binghamton University Milt Kessler Poetry Book Award. Recently, her poem "Surrogate Twin" was selected by Pulitzer-Prize winning poet, Rita Dove, and featured in The New York Times Magazine. Rivera Prosdocimi's work has also appeared in the *Bellevue Literary Review, Cold Mountain Review, Kweli, Nimrod, Poet Lore, Puerto de Sol, The Caribbean Writer, Wasafiri,* and *Witness*. She holds a Ph.D. in Comparative Literature from the University of Maryland and an M.F.A. in Creative Writing from American University. Currently, she teaches literature at the University of Hartford.

ROSINA ROA is an Afro-Latinx with Dominican roots. She was born and raised in Washington Heights, New York City. She uses poetry to spew out thoughts of who she is, what she is, and what is happening around her in the confusing melting pot that is Washington Heights, while also receiving a private education in Downtown New York. Rosina has a BA from Hartwick College in Art History and a Not-For-Profit Financial Management and Reporting certificate from Baruch College. She is currently the Director of Finance and Human Resources at the non-profit organization, Madison Square Park Conservancy. She is currently on the board of Operation Exodus Inner City. This will be the first time she publishes her poetry. Rosina currently resides in Jersey City, NJ.

NI DE AQUÍ, NI DE ALLÁ

YOHELY SALAZAR was born in the Dominican Republic and raised both there and in Massachusetts. Her mission is to live a life of creativity and kindness, while exploring her cultural background through the written word. Salazar has a BA from Williams College in French and French Literature, with a minor in Latino Studies and an AA in Design from the Polimoda Institute in Florence, as well as a BA in Lingerie Design at the Fashion Institute of Technology. She is an itinerant writer and lingerie designer, slowly shifting her focus to more personal works after two years of writing travel pieces for LUXOS magazine, in Milan. She is preparing for her next move at the end of the summer. Yohely is currently based in Los Angeles, California.

CAROLINE SALDANA is a Dominican woman. She was Born and raised in the Bronx. As a young woman, Caroline, always leaned towards helping her neighbors and breaking generational curses on a daily basis. She has made it her mission to educate and learn from her environment in order to expand her horizons. Whether she's helping clean up the streets in her community or working long shifts at the hospital, she has a tremendous love for caring for others. Caroline studied to become a medical assistant and has been in the medical field for 9 years. Her role now is Ophthalmic Technician, where she works alongside board certified ophthalmologists. In the upcoming months, Caroline will return to school for Nursing. After the start of the pandemic, Caroline noticed that her urge to help those in need had grown that much larger. Caroline currently resides in Flushing, NY.

DAFNY SANCHEZ was born and raised in Washington Heights, New York City and is of Dominican heritage. When she is not writing poetry or short fiction stories, you can find her in the kitchen cooking her favorite dishes from the motherland. She caters events for a living, enjoys arts and crafts, and is a spiritual healer.

ANABEL SOTO was born in the Dominican Republic and raised in BedStuy Brooklyn. She amplifies the images and voices of immigrants and people of color through books for children, poetry and flash fiction. Anabel is still adjusting to the biggest promotion and most challenging role of her life—that of mother. Prior to that, Anabel led a carefree life as a beauty editor turned sales executive. When she's not hovering over or dashing after her very own Batgirl and Spiderman, she's enjoying a brief minute of downtime for a gulp of wine. Anabel is a Highlights Foundation Fellow and has performed for PEN America Lit Crawl NYC. Her work has been featured in national publications such as *Health Magazine* and *Seventeen* magazine, the national award-winning magazine *Dollars & Sense*, the literary journal *Encounters*, the *New Voices Anthology* and the *Anthology Ritmo Que Late*. Anabel's debut children's picture book, *Snowy Day* is available on Amazon.

NATASHA SOTO was born and raised in a Dominican-Ecuadorian household in New York City. She is currently an MFA candidate in Creative Writing and an English instructor at Rutgers-Camden University. She received a BA in Latin American Literature and Psychology from Bowdoin College. Her words can be found in *La Galería, Siren Magazine,* and *La Liga Zine.*

JUANA TORIBIO was born in Santiago, Dominican Republic and raised in New York City. Toribio is no stranger to the experience of being "Ni de aquí, Ni de allá." Despite the cultural challenges that come with being una Dominicana Americanizada, Juana maintains the connection to her roots and is raising her vibrant daughter, Ali, with the traditions and language of her Dominican heritage. Juana is a recovering corporate tax accountant. She holds degrees in Accounting and Spanish from Manhattan College in Riverdale, New York, and a certification in Tax Planning from NYU. After dedicating 12 years to Corporate America, her life's path brought her back to her true passion, writing and poetry. This passion was realized during her academic years, throughout which she won numerous writing awards, including various *Daily News* writing contests. Juana Toribio has always been an author at heart.

PALOMA VALENZUELA is a Dominican-American writer, director and actress, originally from the city of Boston. She is the Creative Director of the production operation, La Gringa Loca Productions. She is the writer/producer/creator of the comedic web series, *The Pineapple Diaries.* In 2017 the show was featured in *Latina Magazine's* article, "5 Web Series Every Latinx Needs to Watch Right Now." In 2019, Paloma was featured in *Boston Magazine's* "Boston's New Creative Guard," and selected as one of the WBUR Artery 25, a series highlighting millennials of color making an impact in the Boston arts scene. Paloma has collaborated with the Isabella Stewart Gardner Museum as a museum Neighborhood Salon Artist Luminary. She is the recipient of the 2016 Creative City Grant, the 2018 City of Boston Opportunity Grant, and, in 2019, she was granted the City of Boston Artist Fellowship. In March 2020, Paloma finished editing and launching the third season of *The Pineapple Diaries.* She is currently planning for future projects and has been working as a teaching artist teaching screenwriting and productions for organizations such as GrubStreet, in Boston, and the Institute of Contemporary Art.

SYDNEY VALERIO is a creative non-fiction mixed genre writer and performer. She is a Bronx mother whose family is from Castañuelas. She daylights as an educator & moonlights as a creative. In 2016 she wrote and performed "Matters" a one woman show at the Nuyorican Poets Cafe. Her poetry is in several anthologies including the BreakBeat Poets Vol. 4: Latinext. A 2019 BRIO Award winning poet & a 2020 VOLCANISTA, she is currently working on her first book as a recent graduate of the MFA in Creative Writing program at The City College of New York. She is the project manager for the CCNY MFA Archives as Muse: a Harlem Storytelling project. She is also in the gathering and collecting phase of the Bronx Council on the Arts & NYC Cultural Affairs Department of Arts funded creative digital archive project: Perspective Matters-NYC Kid Who's Now a NYC Adult.

ACKNOWLEDGEMENTS

First and foremost I want to express my gratitude to all the writers who contributed to this compilation, especially for the immense amount of patience they exhibited throughout the editing, designing and publishing of this anthology. Putting together this body of work presented challenges that took some time to resolve, however we persisted and two years from the initial announcement of the call for submissions we can finally push this out to the world.

Thank you to our editors, all five of you who reviewed and revised the manuscript so many times until we it was ready for publishing. Thank you for putting up with my constant requests, and follow-up emails. I hope we can continue working together.

Angela Abreu
Founder/Creative Director
Dominican Writers Association

CPSIA information can be obtained
at www.ICGtesting.com
Printed in the USA
BVHW040219090921
616436BV00014B/533